NOW I SEE

A Walk Through Life's Journey But Never Alone

Lynnie Lang

authorHOUSE®

AuthorHouse™ LLC
1663 Liberty Drive
Bloomington, IN 47403
www.authorhouse.com
Phone: 1-800-839-8640

Published by AuthorHouse 01/15/2014

ISBN: 978-1-4918-4507-3 (sc)
ISBN: 978-1-4918-4510-3 (e)

Library of Congress Control Number: 2013923113

DEDICATED TO

My children, Debbi and David, who are always there for me with much love, support and prayer.

My Grandchildren, Jenni, Jeff, Jesse, Michael, Bianca and Sage, who I love dearly and I pray will carry the love of God to their generation.

My Great Grandchildren, Naomi, Oliver and Silas, who I love dearly and am so grateful God has kept me here long enough to enjoy them.

My family and friends who have loved me through all my human weaknesses, and supported me through the writing of my books.

I am blessed, and I thank God for all of you.

CONTENTS

ACKNOWLEDGMENTS

I extend my gratitude for the support and encouragement expressed to me by the following special people:

Granddaughter Jenni Lynne—Took family pictures for me.

Nothing I do is complete without the touch and love of my Children, Grandchildren and Great Grandchildren.

Andrea—Loyal FL friend for years and supporter of this venture and others God has led me through.

Prudy—Long time close friend who consistently pushed me to keep writing, for some day it was going to be a book. You were right, my friend, here it is!

Jaime—for the excitement we shared working together getting the book ready for publishing. I call her my angel daughter, because I know God brought her into my life.

Ruth from RI—A long time friend who years ago told me I should write a book some day.

Bertie, another encourager who taught me much . . . Counselor and director of a statewide Christian support group, helping those bound in addictions and emotional dependencies of all kinds.

Chaplains Karl and Robbie and friends at Orange County Corrections—appreciation for all the love and support regarding this writing and life itself.

Michele—Who helped me with some of the promotion details and encouraged me as an author.

Author with adoptive parents

CHAPTER I

Divine Revelations of Early Youth

I was born in Providence, Rhode Island on September 2, 1942. I only had the one picture of me as a baby. I spent the first six months with my biological mom and later told I was given to my adoptive parents. On December 31, 1943 this wonderful couple legally adopted me. They were great parents. At times I'd get insecure as adopted children often do. Fearing someone would come and take me away. I would ask, "Do I really belong to you, Mom?" Mom would never tell me or show me adoption papers. She'd say, "You'll see the stuff when I'm dead and gone."

I never knew why she wouldn't show me, until later in my life. Further in my journey I chose to search for a stranger, the need for those adoption papers and more would confront me. I grew up being proud and thankful I was adopted. Dad and Mom could not have a baby of their own, but they always wanted one. Dad told me that when they heard about me needing a home, they knew they wanted me. He said, "We loved you immediately." They didn't change my first name given at birth, and I took on their last name.

My childhood was as normal as any other child's would be. I was popular and had many friends in school and in my neighborhood. Mom and Dad were faithful in bringing me to Sunday school and worship services.

I remember my Godmother, Ruth, calling every Sunday afternoon, if they didn't come to visit. She'd always ask if I'd been to church. It was impressed on me at an early age that it was important to please God and worship Him regularly. This was a foundation that was set, but was only the beginning of God's plan and purpose that is revealed throughout these pages.

High moral standards were also instilled in me. As a teen I had the normal conflicts. Being boy crazy did cause a few. Dad must have been concerned. Quite a few times he warned me not to be permissive with the boys. He'd say, "I don't want you to turn out like your mother. "I had come to the conclusion that he was referring to my biological mother." Guess I must have been born to an unwed mother. I often wondered what reason she had to give me up for adoption. No matter how great your adoptive parents are, some of us still wonder about our biological background.

I also remember Dad telling me that he wished they had adopted another child. He felt bad that I didn't have a brother or sister to grow up with. It seemed to me like there was something missing in my life! I wondered if somewhere in this world I might have a brother or sister. Though I would suppress all this wondering off and on throughout the years ahead, it never stopped the yearning-to-know from returning from time to time. I even fantasized about how my real family might be.

You don't realize till later in life that God's hand is on you as you're growing up. My desire to please God carried me through many difficult decisions that confronted me. Even as a youngster I was a people-pleaser. I'd do anything for anybody thinking it would make them like me better. That can certainly get a teenager in some uncomfortable situations, and did. Boyfriends would try to take advantage of my difficulty in saying no. There is even a friend of the family who took me to *his* basement to "play games" with him.

I am thankful today that my God-consciousness gave me the strength to run from letting things go too far. I would get so uncomfortable and scared. I would finally yell, "God doesn't want us to do this!" Then he would let me go. Often when we're young, we carelessly confuse love with lust. Even at an early age my choices were to please God over pleasing my sinful fleshly desires. Life can be rough. As time went on I learned that difficulties can be for your good and that choices continually affect our lives. I also think it was the fear instilled in me by my Dad. He always warned me not to have a baby like my mother did. All this birth control stuff and the fear of disease weren't making widespread news as it is today.

Those were not the things that kept me from being permissive. Don't get me wrong I was tempted and even desiring to give in many times; yet didn't. I felt the hand of God and His convicting power on me. Thanks to the godly foundation that was laid down for me to live by.

My folks and I had a lot of good times together. Our vacations were great. I loved when we rented a cottage at Jerusalem Beach in Wakefield, RI every summer. It was right on the ocean. Other times we'd stay in Cape Cod, Massachusetts. Mom and Dad's good friends—my godmother Ruth and her husband Ralph—would join us often. They had a son and daughter, Ralph Jr. and Gina. We grew up together. They were very much like a brother and sister to me. In fact Gina was my babysitter when I was a small child.

During most of my growing up yea rs I was surrounded by boys. Another couple my folks were very close to had two sons. Donald later killed himself, due to too much stress in his life, I was told. The other son was Bobby. He was more my age and we got along great. Again, they too seemed as close as brothers to me. Just as I remember Kathy and Lois, my two best child· hood girlfriends. Kathy lived in my neighborhood, across the street from me for about ten years. Jean and Joan were twins, and there were a bunch of boys.

We were all the same age and went to school together. I loved to play with dolls with the girls, and also fit in playing cowboys and Indians with the boys. I was a bit of a tomboy to say the least. It was even difficult for my mom to get me to wear a dress, except for school or church, where slacks were not allowed in those days. I loved my jeans and shorts, and still do. I also loved animals. I can remember always wanting a dog. Mom consistently said I could not have one. One day Dad said to me, "Come along, we're taking a ride." I asked where, and he said it was a surprise. I thought we would never get there, yet it was only a half-hour ride. When you live in the smallest state, a half hour seems far! We ended up at a kennel. I picked out the cutest Cocker Spaniel puppy! I was so excited! I called him Blacky. very original, bet you can guess his color. Of course, in spite of my excitement, I was worried about Mom being upset. Dad said we'd have to tend to that when we got home. He wanted me to have the puppy. He figured Mom would like him when she saw him. Well, just as I thought, she was very upset! She said no way was I going to keep that dog! I was heartbroken. Dad sent me out to the backyard with Blacky while they talked. Let me tell you, I was ready to sleep in the backyard in order to keep my puppy!

How I hated to hear my parents argue over something I wanted. I took it on like it was my entire fault. I wanted to please Mom any way I could and would promise her anything in order to get my way. I started to manipulate at an early age.) Mom and Dad became quiet. Dad didn't come out to take Blacky back. I stayed outside for another hour or so . . . not sure. It seemed like forever! Suddenly Mom stuck her head out the door and said, "You can keep the dog for a few days, and then we'll see." I was both happy, yet scared. Was I going to get to love this new friend and then have to give him up? It would be even more difficult then. I just made up my mind that this puppy was not going to upset Mom. When did a puppy not bother people at some time? Oh well that first night was test #1. I was told to put Blacky outside. Boy did he cry when I left him. I put a stuffed animal, alarm clock, and anything I could think of out there with him. Nothing helped! Mom started yelling that the dog was leaving in the morning!

Dad came to my room. He said, "Go get Blacky and put him on your bed. Just be sure you put him out as soon as he wakes up." Blacky and I went right to sleep and I did as Dad asked in the morning. Dad had told Mom he'd take care of things and he did. Next few days went just as well. Mom found out Blacky was in my room. Since I was taking responsibility for him, she was content in my keeping him. I got through that ordeal and had a wonderful pet for many years. How can an incident with a puppy set a course in life where you end up losing your identity later in life? I would become caught up in a bondage called codependency due to wrong choices. No longer living, but existing. How do you get your life back? Later I will share this nightmare.

My folks were not rich, but comfortable financially. Dad ran his own fabric company. He also worked as a tailor in a company connected with his. Dad and I would go to New York City often to pick up fabric for his store. I loved those trips with him. Dad always spoiled me. He impressed on me that I could have just about anything I wanted; but some things in life you have to learn to wait for. It was great wisdom that I have carried through my adult years. You know, my heavenly Father is like that, too. I've asked Him for answers and things too. Most of the time it seems I have to wait for direction or His yes or no. But, I always get an answer! God too loves to bless His children and knows what is best for us. Most of the time I find He answers when and how I least expect it. It seems I've almost always gotten my way, but I appreciated it and was thankful for what I had.

As I will show you in further chapters, I experienced things and people taken from me. How can being grateful in what you do have, help you through? Now I see how God prepared me for the things in life I was to encounter.

Chapter II

Family Relationships-
Gains and Losses

Let me tell you a little more about my family. I grew up very close to my Aunt Alice. She was Mom's only sister. She had three children, Sharon, Raymond and Bobby, all younger than I. Aunt Alice was divorced when her children were young. I spent a lot of time with her helping with my cousins. I grew up feeling a responsibility towards my cousins. I may mention them again later. My Aunt Alice was more like a second mother than an aunt to me. Mom and I got along Okay, but there was never much affection shared between us. I don't ever remember any mother-daughter serious talks either. I was allowed to give her hugs and a kiss once in a while. Yet they were never returned or given freely on her part.

Dad was the affectionate one, or else I probably would have starved for it. One of his favorite reminders to me was "always be you." Never be afraid to express how you feel about someone. If you love them, tell them and show them. It wasn't till later that I realized Mom wasn't affectionate or loving to Dad either. She had a difficult struggle going through menopause. She'd get very short tempered. I can remember her yanking my hair and throwing things at me. She would lose it over the smallest issues. I loved her very much though, and I know she loved me in her own way. We still had many wonderful and fun times as a family.

Mom taught me that commitment and family were very important. I saw my folks work things out through 25 years of marriage. Dad had five brothers and two sisters. The only times I ever saw him get argumentative was with his brothers and sisters. With Mom, it was only if he had been socially drinking and had a little too much. That wasn't very often. I hated it when it happened though. The Lang Family was a bunch that loved to get into deep discussions. They would get very loud, all trying to prove their points with one another. Yet it was a close knit family. I was always made to feel I was an important part of Dad's family. Being family-oriented proved advantageous later in life, as it brought a desire to help others. Troubled teens, 42 to be exact, came through our home within seven years. Troubles, challenges and blessings for seven years!

When I was 17 years old, Dad took very ill with lung cancer. It was a difficult time for me. Mom was not emotionally fit to "be there" for him. I can remember nights when I slept with his pain pills under my pillow for fear he'd take the whole bottle. He suffered terribly. Little did I know that this most difficult time was preparation for my future in working with folks recovering from all types of addictions and illnesses. I graduated from high school and Dad made it to see me on that special day.

I had some great friends I will never forget: Carol, Peggy and Anne. We joined and were in an Air Force

Auxiliary together. We made some wonderful memories and stuck together for years. We've moved to different states now. Carol and I are still close friends. She was maid of honor at our wedding. We have visited one another over the years. God has just made the way for us to see each other at various times. Though we're miles from each other our visits still happen. It is always a fun time. We feel like kids again until we look at each other and reality sets in!

About this time I was engaged to a great guy who was in the Air Force. He was stationed in California. It was very difficult trying to plan to marry the man I was in love with; and knowing I was losing the man I loved all my life: knowing that it could happen at any time. Ken, my fiance, was away, but we communicated constantly. His family and mine were very supportive in getting the plans made. Dad would say he wanted me to go ahead with my life. He needed to know his little girl was happy and content before he had to leave her. Ken and I were very much in love. I knew he was stable and responsible. After all, I got to know his family. His mom and dad, sister and family were the most wonderful people I've known. We all became very close.

I remember thinking about some day having Ken's children. I would get excited; it was such a sincere desire. I always dreamed of having a big family. Ken came home for our wedding. Dad was too sick to give me away, so my uncle stepped in. It broke Dad's heart and mine for him not to participate in his daughter's special day. What was worse, I knew I was leaving Dad to live in California. It was a very exciting and happy time in my life, yet sad too. The wedding was beautiful. After the ceremony, the whole wedding party went to my parent's home to visit Dad. We also visited Ken's grandma who was also too feeble to attend. We said our good-byes, very difficult; then we were on our way. Our honeymoon consisted of traveling across country back to California. That's military life for you. This was only the beginning of my travels during this journey of my life.

A few months passed and Ken was told he was to be transferred to France. I was then pregnant with our first baby. We didn't feel we wanted our baby born in a foreign country, so I left to come home to Rhode Island. I moved back in with my parents. Dad's cancer had arrested for a time. He had good days and bad. He was excited about the new baby that was coming. I think that is what made him hang on.

September 19, 1962 Debbi Anne was born. What a joy! The two men in my life were so proud and thankful. Of course, I was thrilled to be a mother and to be blessed with this beautiful daughter. MyMom could hardly believe she was a grandmother. They both loved her very much. Dad got to spend over a year with his grand daughter. Ken couldn't get home from France until Debbi was three months old. Sometimes life certainly can be filled with mixed emotions! This was training ground for all the ups and downs life brought me through. Ken finally got home and we could be a family at last.

In November 1963 I was watching TV. It was two days after President Kennedy was shot and killed. I was watching his funeral when I got a call from Mom. Dad had died. He wasn't suffering anymore. Even if you seem prepared, it is never easy to lose a parent. I only wish I knew the Lord as I know Him now. I didn't know how to lean on Him in troubled times. He is always there to comfort us. We are unable to reach out for the Holy Spirit's comfort when we have not allowed Jesus to be Lord of our lives. I did have some wonderful friends and family who were there for me, but this was not easy. I believe this experience helped me when another very tragic event happened to me later in my life.

December 9, 1964, almost one year to the day Dad died, God blessed us with our son, David William. I remember saying to the doctor that it looked like my first baby only a little bigger. The doctor said tl1is one had a little extra! It was a boy! I said, "Oh my, how on earth do I raise a boy?" I never was one, so I guess I wasn't sure how you'd raise one. That's why they have daddies. It was a joy and blessing raising our children.

They were raised to know Jesus Christ as their personal Savior. Of course, this was after I was led to Him in 1970. Let me tell you just how that came about.

Chapter III

Salvation-Inner Healing

Our family life brought many joys, but also heartaches. My husband was a wonderful provider, yet in many areas we did not meet one another's needs. I became very ill when I was about 25 years old. I had developed a terminal blood disease. Two small children at home, and I am in the intensive care unit of a hospital. There was nothing more the doctors could do. They were waiting to see if the blood clots would dissolve or kill me. An elderly lady in a bed across from me spoke to me about Jesus. She said that God loved me so much that he sent His only son to die for my sins. He knows we are all sinners in need of a Savior.

She told me He was reaching out to me through her to accept Him as my Lord and Savior. He would come into my heart and give me new life in Him. He desires to renew the dead spirit within me (dead because of sin) and send His Holy Spirit to cleanse me. She also said she felt I was going to take her place in the church. Oh, not a particular denominational church or not even the church she attended. She meant "the church" (God's redeemed people). Those who receive Jesus Christ as their personal Savior and desire God's will for their lives. She also knew I was the last person she'd be privileged to introduce to her best friend, Jesus.

Well, I didn't quite understand all she was saying, except I heard new life. At that point I knew I didn't have much life left in me. She prayed a beautiful prayer out loud to me asking God to heal me both spiritually and physically. Let my heart be softened to receive Him as my Lord. She reassured me He would answer prayer. Even if I died I'd have the assurance of having eternal life with Christ. One way or the other you are healed of the suffering and pain. When He is Lord of your life, you have the hope and promise of John 3:16. "For God so loved the world (you), that He gave His only begotten Son, that whosoever believes in Him shall not perish, but have everlasting life." She became very tired and said for me to ponder her words in my mind and heart. They are truth and the truth will set you free.

I want to tell you, there was no sleep for me, at first that night. I wrestled with thoughts for quite some time. Thoughts like, "Won't you receive me as your Lord? I love you, my child, and long to help you. Call on me and I will answer you." I didn't understand. Was this really God communicating with me in my mind? A part of me wrestled, another part of me wanted so much to know God as Julia knew Him. She seemed so peaceful knowing she was ready to die. She was looking forward to seeing Jesus. She actually seemed to glow as she spoke to me. I lay there unable to sleep. Finally, I remember beginning to talk with God like I never had before. It seems like it was yesterday as I write about it now. I said, "God (didn't know Him as Lord yet) there isn't much left of me to give you. Yes, I am a sinner and so undeserving. I want to know You like Julia knows You. Please forgive me and come into my life. I want you to be Lord of my life."

Ephesians 2:8,9 says "For by grace are ye saved through faith: and that not of yourselves: it is the gift of God; Not of works, lest any man should boast." Well, nothing spectacular happened except I fell asleep. I slept through the night, which was very rare because I would always wake up in pain. The nurses were even amazed. They said they had checked on me several times and I was sleeping like a baby. I should also mention that my left leg was swollen twice the size of my right one. The doctors wouldn't allow me out of my bed. I couldn't even feed myself for fear any movement would dislodge a blood clot to my heart and kill me.

Well, I tell you, I woke up that next morning with no pain! I was so shocked! I knew God had touched me and began to thank Him for how I felt. I climbed out of bed to go tell the nurses about my miracle. They hurried me back to bed and were ready to call the psychiatrist! I told them to look at my leg. It was normal size and I had no pain in my leg or chest. TI1ey knew I never had relief from either without constant medication. I hadn't had any medication since the night before! I insisted they get the doctor here soon because I wanted to go home. The nurses were quite amazed at what they saw. They really didn't understand, but had to admit something out of the ordinary had happened.

I knew there was someone who would understand: Julia. I looked over towards her bed. Her curtain was drawn. It seemed that a nurse was tending to her. I called to her excitedly. The nurse came out from behind the curtain to come over to me. She told me Julia had died. All I could do was cry. I wanted her to know. Then it seemed that a quiet, calming thought as if from God said, "She knows." I felt my spirit well up inside me with joy and thanksgiving.

Surely she knew and she had the confidence that God's Word does not return void. She knew He had already prepared my heart to receive His word from her. That is why she could let go and leave this world behind. She knew there was a better place prepared for her. I knew then that I also desired to tell· others about Jesus. Everybody needs Jesus in his or her life! My life has never been the same since and I thank God for that. I was completely healed. The doctors were amazed. They wrote in their books that I was a true miracle. "Therefore if any man be in Christ he is a new creature; old things are passed away; behold all things are become new." 2 Corinthians 5:17.

What follows is the beginning of a transformation of my life. I allowed God to work in my life and you will see His intervention. Wrong choices brought me devastating circumstances that I thought were irreversible. Facing life and death situations with nowhere to turn. Could I really trust God? Does God really care about all the details of my life?

CHAPTER IV

Spiritual Growth through Life's Trials

As you will see my life took on a whole new direction: the path God had purposed for me from the beginning. He changed my life for the better. It didn't mean perfect, just forgiven. It didn't mean I never got sick again or never had any more problems. No way. Life goes on with all its difficulties. The big difference is that my God is bigger than any problem and is able to carry me through. I didn't always do what God wanted me to do either, I'm sure. He began to work in my life because I chose to let Him.

I never had a problem with my blood again, though the symptoms would come and go for about eight more months. Prior to this I found a great church. I learned about the power of prayer. Acknowledging that Satan, the god of this world, lies to God's people continually. He lies to the people he has won to himself as well, in order to get them to do what he wants them to do. This is always contrary to God's way and will for their lives. How we need to stand on the Word of God. "In the beginning was the Word and the Word was with God and the Word was God. The Word became flesh and dwelt among us, and we beheld His glory, the glory as of the only begotten of the Father, full of grace and truth." John 1:1+14.

I learned we can stand on God's word and in the name of Jesus there is power. We have power over the enemy of our souls, power from God through Jesus Christ, not of ourselves. Spiritual authority in Jesus' name to kick the devil out of our lives and demand he leave us alone! I prayed every time the symptoms returned; and they had to leave and did. Our battle in this world is a spiritual one, but few realize that. We have allowed Satan to have many strongholds in our lives that he has no rights to. I know that without child-like faith and the knowledge of God's power; I would not have overcome life's battles.

When your life is in God's hands you can trust He will bring you through all difficulties. I didn't say He'd bring you past them or over them or around them. He brings us through them with victory on the other side.

We learn and mature spiritually with each experience. His Holy Spirit working in and through us renews our spirits. Just as a child with simple faith trusts her daddy to help her through everything, we too can have that confidence. Although their earthly parent has forsaken some, our heavenly Father says in Hebrews 13:5, "I will never leave thee, nor forsake thee." As Jesus said to His disciples when He called a little child unto Him in the midst of them; "Verily I say unto you, except you be converted and become as little children, you shall not enter into the kingdom of heaven." (Matthew 18:3)

My family put our lives in God's hands and asked Him to have His way. We desired to do His will. Our lives continually moved forward from then on. We settled in a Baptist church; which also affiliated with a Pentecostal church frequently. Little did we know or have any idea what we were going to be up against later down the road. We were still young in our walk with God. I was hungry to know all I could about this spiritual walk. Not really aware that it is also a warfare. Satan does not like to lose one soul to Jesus. He'll do all he can to get you back. I was diligently in God's word, and watched and listened to my elders in the church. You can learn from those who have "been there." There was one precious lady in particular. I called her Grandma Balcom. She loved the Lord so much and was a great encouragement to me. If God puts an older godly person in your life consider yourself blessed.

Let me tell you more. I learned right quick that pastors are not infallible. The church had a beautiful fellowship of believers and was growing. All seemed to be going well, and we were growing spiritually as well. Then I began to sense something was wrong. My daughter was only about seven years old, but she also became uncomfortable with the pastor's behaviors. Not an easy place to be in. I spoke with Debbi and suggested we should just pray for him. I also shared privately with Grandma Balcom, and she agreed something was going wrong. She explained that we were spiritually discerning a wrong spirit trying to take over through pride and lust. We prayed and continued in prayer that either he would come to it himself or that it would show itself. We wanted God to have His way with this whole situation. The fellowship became a love cult with the pastor leading it as it being God's love he was demonstrating! It started with passionate kissing.

I finally confronted him and was excommunicated from the church. My family left and so did Grandma Balcom. No one else followed. I was so burdened for them. How we can be deceived by the devils lies and schemes! I thanked God for His power and grace to stand against the forces of evil. Again it is still difficult to make choices that will result in losing some wonderful friends. Especially knowing you are leaving them in the hands of Satan's disciple. Yet if they cannot or will not see or hear the truth, you have no choice. We quickly became active in another church and soon were led to move to Seattle, Washington: another experience to tell you about.

We lived in a huge home with thirty other people. It was certainly a mission field. We were trained to counsel troubled young people. It was also a spiritual training ground for all of us working there. God seemed to be working on us as we worked with others. Several months later I began to hear from the folks from the church that had fallen. Through prayer, they had finally seen the truth and left. I was informed that the pastor was eventually forced out of that city and his ministerial rights taken from him. What a great God we serve. When we pray He breaks down the strongholds of Satan, even from thousands of miles away. There is truly power in prayer!

Let me go into more of our Seattle events. I know I have mentioned my cousins, Sharon, Ray and Bobby: those I felt responsibility for as I was growing up. Well, word came to us that my Aunt Alice died of a heart attack while shoveling snow back in Rhode Island.

Let me explain something here. My cousins had emotional and behavioral problems. Two of them were educationally slow. Sharon had had a baby and lived with the father for only a short time. My aunt was the one taking care of the child. I had to fly back to RI to help my mom with the funeral arrangements, and placement of my aunt's children. Bobby was going to stay with a ·friend of his, an older gentleman. I ended up bringing Sharon and the baby back to Seattle.

It wasn't very long when I realized Sharon was having difficulty caring for the child emotionally. She became abusive and she didn't know why. I talked with her about what would be best for her child and her. After much prayer and counseling she agreed it would be best to give him up for adoption. Since she knew I was adopted and how happy my life was, she was not afraid for him. It was one of the most difficult things I ever did. It was heart-rending to see a mother and child separated. I had prayed so hard for God's wisdom and strength for that whole situation.

Chapter V

God's Commission Back in Our Home State

It came time for us to move back to Rhode Island. We were not home long before we were settled back in another church. I will always remember the first young lady God sent to us from the church we were attending. Word quickly reached the churches in our area that we were back and how God was going to use us. Really even before we knew for sure. I remember, as if it were yesterday, what this young lady said to me as she stood at my door. "My pastor sent me to see you. I don't feel that anyone, especially God, could ever love me after what I have done."

That was the beginning of the ministry God used us in for seven years. We saw 42 troubled teenage girls move through our home-lives committed to Jesus Christ as their Lord and Savior. We saw them transformed by the renewing power of God's Holy Spirit, transformed from troubled street kids to God's young ladies. Eventually even the state juvenile detention center was sending girls they thought our program could help. Soon the state stepped in and chartered us as the "Christian Home For Girls." There were a few who sensed the pull in the world was too strong and they left our home too early. This caused them to fall back into their old ways.

They could leave whenever they wanted to. We always encouraged them to stay in fellowship with other Christians, attend a bible preaching church, pray and read the bible daily. Without a foundation, structure and godly guidelines we dry up spiritually. Satan comes in like a roaring lion to seek whom he can devour. When we do not stay built up in the faith, we become prey to the adversary, the devil. "Know ye not, that to whom ye yield yourselves servants to obey, his servants you are to whom ye obey; whether of sin unto death, or of obedience unto righteousness." (Romans 6:16) God has a wonderful purpose for our lives if we desire His will.

More came from our stay in Seattle, Washington than we'd ever imagined. I had come home with a burning desire to be part of a Christian woman's fellowship called AGLOW. I quickly found out there wasn't such a thing in RI. I spoke with several friends of mine to see how they felt about getting one started. They were very interested. We began to pray for God's direction. I remember calling the president of the Full Gospel Businessman's Fellowship, who was then Brother Nash, a wonderful man of God. I asked him for some ideas on how to get a woman's group started. He prayed with me and then gave me some guidelines and direction.

We started with a get-together for discussion. There were six women and myself present. Each woman had her individual God-given talents. It was amazing how God had already placed us in each others lives for this purpose. One was experienced and good at handling money; she stepped into the treasurer position. Another had great musical abilities, another secretarial experience; and so on as each position for the executive board was filled. *All* was decided, except president. It seemed everyone knew God called me to be the president except me. I just thought I was getting it started! Honestly I felt like Moses. Definitely not qualified to head a statewide Christian women's fellowship.

I had always hesitated to accept any leadership positions. God knew this would be the only way I'd know He called me to do this. Yes, and He gave me the ability to carry the position for one year! What a privilege, challenge and spiritual growth experience it was for me. I was blessed and thankful for the wonderful staff God had given me. We were a team for the Lord's work. It is still going on today. I am grateful I listened and heeded God's call to begin Woman's Aglow Fellowship of RI. I know many women and their families have been encouraged and enriched because of the dedication of those women who have kept it going all these years. After a year I resigned to allow someone else to serve as president and be blessed as I was.

Back at home our own children were into their teens now. I began to feel it was time to devote more time to my husband and children. Our home ministry also closed. It was a great privilege to have been used to teach others of God's desire to be active in their lives, praying always for His direction for them and still do. I believe we are all in need of a higher power, God, as we see Him in our own individual way. We all need to seek Him privately. Accepting Him as Lord of our life and allowing Him to direct our path in life is so important.

I know how easy it is to go our own way, but it always trips us up and we fall or fail. The important thing is to get up and start over. It's a new day with new discoveries and new challenges!

Chapter VI

Family Life's Joys and Heartaches

My life with my first husband, Debbi and Dave's father, brought many joys. We also had our heartaches. Isn't that what life is all about anyway? That is why we have such a patient, understanding God watching over us. Our choices in life are just that, our choices. Whether good or bad results, I believe God uses them to teach others and us as we live our choices out. I've come to realize and question, is there really a wrong choice we can make? Yes, if it does not measure up with God's will for us. He knows we are human and we are limited, as much as we try, to always make right choices. Why do I find it so difficult to just let go and let God take over?

I always think I have to do it all myself. He wants to take part in all our choices in life. Why do we fight against letting God take complete control? Life is so much easier when we are in His divine will. I speak from experience believe me. Most of the time I find myself running my life, my way. I am the one who makes my life difficult.

Again in my life I made another big choice. I decided to go back to college and become a nurse. I did it. God knew, even if I didn't, that I was going to need a career to fall back on. Even before I graduated, God interceded with a plan for my future. During my hospital training, I was privileged to look in on eye surgery being performed. The surgeon was so impressed with my interest in what he was doing; he asked to speak with me later. He asked what my plans were after I graduated. I had none. He said he'd like to hire me and put me through extended ophthalmic nurse training. He and his sister, an optometrist, would then teach me how to assist in running his office. I worked for him for many years. His name is Dr. Paul Koch. He is the best eye surgeon I know. They were a wonderful family to work for; his dad worked there also. They made their employees feel like we were part of the family.

I'd like to tell you one more thing about nursing school. My daughter was also attending the same college. We took some courses together. Boy was that ever fun! I remember it was daughter-helping-mom with homework, more than the other way around. Becoming a nurse was blessing number one. The day I graduated I was informed of blessing number two. My daughter told me I was to become a grandmother! Talk about double blessings! When my Debbi graduated, we have pictures of her in cap and gown with baby Jenni on her lap. All that was the beginning of my nursing career and Debbi's mothering days, which are still going on today with four more children!

It is difficult to think back to sad times. I know I must when it may help someone reading this. Over the years my husband got addicted to prescription drugs. It all began with migraine headaches. Our relationship and family suffered through at least ten years of the almost twenty-five we were together. Five of those years I kept his secret from our children. Trying to spare them.

Saying Dad was sick. That was why he acted so different at times. I even lied to myself. I didn't want to believe it either.

A relationship dead, due to drug abuse; prescription or street drugs cause destruction to both the person addicted and all those close to them. Knowing what I know now, I probably should have walked away. It might have spared our children and myself some of the difficulties we experienced. It might have also gotten him help earlier. I stayed, trying to be the good wife. I wanted to be faithful to the end, end of what, his life or mine? We now had a dead relationship. Hurting emotionally, mentally, physically and spiritually. It takes its toll in every part of you.

Yet we stay, why? Why is it so difficult to walk away from things and people who are causing us distress, heartache or any form of abuse? Is it guilt, pride, fear, shame, remorse, stubbornness, dedication? Is it a combination of them all? Still we have a choice and do not make it. We do not have to allow anyone to make us feel uncomfortable or cause us pain. Some of us take years to learn to make the right choices for ourselves. I'm still learning to make choices that are good for me. I hope-and pray this book will encourage someone to make good choices early in their life.

My husband and I were married nearly twenty-five years. Many times he told me to get out of his life. I became a threat to his addiction. Being a nurse, I knew all the signs. Of course, I denied it for as long as I could stand it. I began to call the doctors that were on his prescriptions. That forced them to stop supplying them. Especially when they realized he had several doctors supplying the same type of medications. Tough love is a difficult thing to administer. It can come across as hate to the substance abuser. My husband became very angry and abusive both verbally and physically. It is difficult to suffer the consequences of finally doing something to change things in order to save your own sanity.

Yet inside you know it is best for both of you and the family. So with God's help I did whatever it took in hope he would get the help he needed. But, the opposite can happen and we must be ready to accept that also. I wasn't. It wasn't very long when he realized his doctors were taking him off the heavy pain medications. He panicked and became violent with me. He forced me out of the house and out of his life. I was both distraught and relieved to be away from him. I always believed I married for life, for better or worse. I believed my vows and would have never left him.

I realize now God does not expect us to become martyrs for our husbands or anyone. We are human; we are individuals and deserve to be treated right. I knew I wouldn't be returning until we both got some help; yet I was fearful of going on alone. Our children were grown. Our daughter, Debbi was married then. I also knew I would have to suffer the consequences of how they would take all this. Knowing their Dad was still in denial about his addiction and me not staying by him to help him like I always did. How could I expect them to understand? I always appeared to be the strong one. Only because I leaned on the Lord for my strength to endure the hardship I chose to stay a part of. Sometimes we think we have to stay together for the sake of our children or because of the vows we took. Yet there are times when all parties can be deeply harmed by staying together in substance abuse relationships.

Now I see we make choices to stay in a relationship because it brings us joy, peace, happiness, and contentment. I now believe it is insane to stay in a relationship that does not enrich the parties involved. Without good counsel and allowing God's intervention to change you, things only continue to get worse. It has taken me 54 years and three close relationships to finally come to this realization and conclusion. As I said, I am still recovering and learning to make right choices for myself. I'm sure I will always be learning, but hopefully not so much by my mistakes.

Let me go on and tell you what happened next. I find myself out and alone. Never in my life had I been on my own. I've never been one to lean on my children. They have their own lives to live. I spoke with each of them and reassured them I would be okay. I tried to explain that Dad didn't want me in his life anymore. Not realizing, of course, that he was going to deny that to them. I knew then that I was going to have to trust God that some day they would learn the truth. I just asked that they would just love us both through this because we both loved them very much.

I stayed with a friend that first night and went to work from there the next day. Praying for God's direction because I did not know what I was to do next,

I talked with a friend at work. She suggested I stay at a campground till I saw where my life was going. God will put people in your life to direct you His way, believe me. He knows whom we need to be with when we ask Him to take over our lives. I picked up the phone book to look for a campground. Not even knowing if there was one that may have campers to rent.

One campground stood right out to me. It was in Scituate, RI, 20 miles from work. It was located out in the country, quiet and peaceful. It was exactly what I needed at the time.

A very kind gentleman answered the phone. He said he didn't rent trailers out, then asked what I needed. I told him my dog and I needed a place to live as soon as possible. He proceeded to tell me he'd like to fix a spot for me overlooking the lake! He had a small camper that needed a good cleaning that I could rent. I felt so blessed. Here this man had no idea who I was; yet he wanted to help me. I had no idea what this was going to be like, but I trusted God had it all figured out for me and I'd be O.K.

I have some wonderful friends, Dr. Richard Belhumeur, a RI optometrist friend, and his wife Barbara. Barbara went with me to clean the trailer. It was filthy, but with much effort we got it sparkling. I was able to stay in it that night. Isn't God good? It was a beautiful area. I spent the summer there. My daughter and grandchildren visited often. We had some fun times at the lake. It was like a vacation as I made the adjustments necessary to get my life back.

Meanwhile God had another miracle about to happen. A friend from work decided to sell his 34-foot house trailer. He asked if I'd be interested. I went to see it and it was beautiful. It would be perfect for me. Yet I didn't have any credit established in my name, so I had no idea how I was going to purchase it. He offered to go to his bank and do all he could for me to buy it. All went well and it was mine! He even had it moved to my campsite. The owner of the campground assisted in my move. He was so happy for me. He was a wonderful, considerate gentleman. His wife was always sending him out to make sure I was 0kay. especially if the weather was bad. I stayed there for another month when some more changes came into my life.

CHAPTER VII

Difficult Adjustments Bring Spiritual Growth

Seven miles from where I worked, I found a mobile home park. They said I could rent a lot and put my trailer on it. I was so excited! a purpose for me moving there. His direction may not always be clear to us. That is why it is a faith walk when we trust God. As we trust Him it becomes evident what we are to do. If there is ever a lesson I've learned, and am still learning to apply, it is that *when in doubt, don't do it.* God is a God of peace. Peace enters in when it is what He wants you to do. Yet there are still times when I choose to jump ahead of Him and do my own thing. You know, even those times He uses for me to learn by.

I moved and living there was wonderful. Much transpired during my stay there. Let me fill you in on some more of my life. You will see how God always kept *His* hand on me. I met a wonderful couple that lived next door. They were great Christian neighbors all the time I lived there. I was always active in my church, usually in the music ministry or helping folks in need. I am a self-taught guitar player. I loved visiting nursing homes. The senior citizens and I would sing praises to our Lord together. I would go to be a blessing to them and they would end up blessing me, telling me stories of how God worked miracles in their lives.

Years passed and I was content. I had my little home I could call my own. My dear friends, Carl and Linda had their own construction business. They built an addition onto my trailer. It gave me a nice size living room. It was comfortable and cozy. I was still working as an eye surgery nurse. I worked with a wonderful staff that were also my friends. After seven years of being alone, I met this wonderful gentleman. He was a patient at the eye doctor's where I worked. I'll never forget the first words he said to me, "Why are all the beautiful women taken?" What a line, I thought. But he was as sincere as he could be. I then realized he was reaching out to me in his own sweet way.

I also knew I was attracted to him with his shiny white hair and gentle manner. That day grew to dinner out together, walks down at the ocean and many other great sharing times. Our love and commitment for each other began to grow. In July 7, 1990 we were married. We went to Prince Edward Island for a two-week honeymoon. It was a wedding gift from Uncle John and Norma. Uncle John was our neighbor in RI for many years when I was growing up. He also owned a cottage on the island and that was where he let us stay. This was another blessing from the Lord.

Richard and I always tried to keep Christ the center of our relationship. He was a fisherman all his life and now was semi-retired. He has six children, all grown. Everyone was happy to see the love we shared with each other; never to imagine what was down the road for us.

Life can hit us with difficulties very unexpectedly, no warning and no time to prepare ourselves. I guess it's best that way. God knows some happenings you could never be prepared for even if you tried.

Rich had been acting differently lately, even strangely at times. I noticed his words slurring, loss of his balance and more frequent sleeping. Also he was short-tempered with himself. I had never seen him like this before. Since my first marriage became abusive, Rich and I had promised to never hurt each other verbally or otherwise. We were always able to talk about anything with each other. When I'd ask him if something were wrong, he'd say, "Nothing, Love, I'm just fine, a bit tired maybe." He didn't seem to notice anything different about himself. I still suggested he go to the doctors for a check up. He went. The doctor said he was as healthy as someone ten years younger.

Comments like that made Rich feel great. Especially when at times he felt like he robbed the cradle marrying me. He knew I loved being his wife and I loved how he loved me. Then one night the nightmare happened: We were married six months now. I came home from work, and Rich was on the floor! I thought he was dead! I checked him my heart pounding! I was able to arouse him, thank God. He began to hit and kick me. I panicked and tried to calm him, but I was getting hurt. I tried to run to the phone to call 911. He managed to get up and grab me. He socked me in the face. I saw fear in his face and it scared me.

He was very strong, and I was definitely getting hurt badly. By now he had me by the throat. I managed to get my strength and balance, lifted my leg to his stomach and pushed him real hard. He lost his balance and fell. I ran out of the house and down the street bleeding and crying. I said to myself, "this can't be happening, this is not my Richard!" I got to my neighbor's trailer; they were home, thank God. I hurriedly told them something terrible has happened to my husband. They could see I was hurt, and were confused why I was concerned for Rich. They called the police. I met the police outside and asked them to please get an ambulance for my husband. One officer stayed outside with me. The other one went in to Richard. After a few minutes, no ambulance came. The other officer was called inside to assist. I waited outside. Both officers came out with Richard being practically carried out between them in handcuffs! They put him in the car, and one of the officers took him to j ail!

The other officer stayed with me to try to explain some things. I was confused and upset. I kept telling the officer that Rich was sick. He said, "Ma'am, he assaulted you, we could see that. He is totally intoxicated." He said they would check him further when he got to the station. I was devastated, confused, scared and very upset by now. Was I trying to deny a truth about Richard, I didn't want to face? Would I be able to let him back into my life after this?

I didn't hear anything for a few days. His son called to tell me he was out of jail and in a hotel. He wanted to come home. I told him I was afraid of him, and gave him his clothes. I asked! Jim to. give me some time to pray and heal from all this. Two nights later a policeman was at my door. A car had struck my husband as he was crossing the street. He informed me that he was still alive, but it didn't look good. How could this be? Everything was happening too fast for me. The time was 8:30 p.m. They explained to me that Richard might have been trying to cross the street when an intoxicated driver hit him. Richard's daughter and I went to the hospital. His sons joined us. The doctors informed us that Richard was brain dead; that there was no hope of recovery. If he lived, he'd be a vegetable.

Each time I would talk with him, through the night, his heartbeat would get stronger on the monitor. It was agony listening to his heart beat get slower and slower as the night slowly dragged on. Near dawn I felt impressed to tell Rich that it was 0.K. to let go if God was calling him home. I told him I forgave him and that I loved him very much. I would miss him, but I knew God did not want him to struggle in this life anymore. Moments later he let go, and went home to be with the Lord.

His daughter later told me she thought maybe he was drinking again and didn't want me to know. That was what broke his first marriage up, alcoholism. I knew that, but I had never seen Rich drink any alcoholic beverage. I will never know what really happened the night he got killed. Maybe I'm not even supposed to try to guess what happened, or maybe I am in denial still. I would rather just remember Richard for the wonderful man I married. I thank God for the time He gave me with him. All the beautiful times we had together seem to erase the brief traumatic struggles we shared before his life was ended so tragically.

Chapter VIII

Our Past Preparation for the Future

I have always believed that when God closes one door He opens another. Maybe not right away but as we heal and seek His will, life seems to once again open up to us and take on new meaning.

I decided to change jobs, not career, just my nursing field. I wanted to only work four days a week now for a while. I needed more time to myself. I prayed for guidance and felt God leading me to a doctor's office close to my home. Sure enough, I began working for an allergy specialist, Dr. Anthony Ricci Let me tell you, God has always put me with the best doctors to work for. Dr. Ricci and the staff I worked with were great. They were not only fellow employees; they became precious friends I will never forget. It was quite an experience and privilege to be able to train in a totally different field of nursing. Only with God's help and Dr. Ricci's good teaching and patience, did I accomplish it!

Well, are you ready to hear about another miracle in my life? Here goes! Many times in my lifetime, I desired to know who my birth mother was, as you have heard me say before. I was also curious to know if I had any brothers and sisters. For one reason or another I never went anywhere with the idea of . . . searching for them while my adoptive folks were still alive. I would never want to hurt them for anything. By the way, my adopted mom had a fatal stroke about fifteen years after dad died. After I lost my adopted mom, I did get the desire to search for my biological mom, yet I had my family, and that was enough to keep me busy and content.

When you are an adopted child you always wonder about your family background. You know nothing about your medical history or who you might look like, etc. Somehow it always feels like a part of your life is missing. You know nothing about the real you, who you really came from or where you were born. Some adopted folks don't care to know. I always wondered. I even fantasized about having brothers and sisters, since I was brought up as an only child. I think that was why my girlfriends were very special to me. I especially remember Kathy and Lois when I was a youngster, and Carol, Peggy and Anne when I was a teen. Liz, Debbie, Barbara and Linda were all like sisters to me in Rl. To this day I cherish those friendships. I am still in touch with some of them.

Let me back-track again before I tell how my miracle came about. I want to tell you a little more about myself. I always seem to love people too much if that can be-always had a tendency to please people any way I could. Often my expressions of love and affection were taken the wrong way. Even when I dated, the guys would take my love and affection to mean I wanted more. Yet my heart was right before God and I never wanted to hurt Him.

Recently I read a book, "Women Who Love Too Much" written by Robin Norwood. I had never realized that loving too much could hurt you and others and even destroy you! Now don't get me wrong, we can never love God too much. The enemy of our souls, Satan, is always there to use and abuse the love we have in our hearts. He can use it for a tool for sin if we do not always guard ourselves. We need to keep our minds and bodies pure before God for God's love is pure.

Maybe all my life I felt I needed to love my mom so much because it seemed that she didn't know how to love. Mom and I were not close until the last five years of her life. She accepted Christ as her Lord and Savior. Before then, she was distant, not a very warm person. Yet, inside I felt she loved me. She must have, after all she was my mother! I could show her affection, but I don't ever remember her returning it. I believe this leaves scars. A child needs their mother's affection and loving touch, no matter what age and for as long as she may live.

God placed mother, brother and sister substitutes in my life. Some who seem to fill a void in my life were my Aunt Lillian Lang and our neighbor, Blanche Lester. When I was a teenager I remember a wonderful lady, Ruth Vallone. I babysat for her children. She was a wonderful influence in my life. In fact she is one who encouraged me to write a book some day. She gave me the tools to get started. I am putting them to good use. My rough draft has been hand written in a loose-leaf book that she gave me. I could talk with her so easily about anything. She is a very warm, loving person. She always expressed genuine, unconditional love and affection. I wanted to be like her when I got older, an encouragement and an inspiration to the younger generation. God knew my desire and brought all those foster teens into my life. It takes commitment and dedication to God's will to be used of God for others, not perfection. God knew I wasn't perfect. I still made mistakes and fell short many times. That is why I am so thankful for God's forgiveness. For if we fail God, as I feel I have at times, He is willing and ready to forgive and forget. He desires for us to do the same for ourselves and go on. He does want us to learn and grow by our mistakes, though. I certainly have and will continue to do so.

CHAPTER IX

'Thanks Mom for Letting Me Live'

I said all the previous to begin to tell you about my long awaited search for my biological Mom and siblings if there were any. I really didn't know where to begin my search for a "stranger." All I had was a name. My search began with prayer and continued in prayer, as you will see. This was September, 1991: I had found my adopted Mom's strongbox after she died. In it was my adoption decree. I then knew I really did legally belong to them. I also realized why Mom never wanted me to see those papers. My birth Mom's name was on it and my last name at birth.

In June, while at work, I met a gentleman with the same last name as my birth name, which was Jenkins. I asked if he knew a Marylin Jenkins. He said she was his sister in-law many year ago. Everyone had lost contact with her when she and his brother divorced. Boy, how you can get excited and hit a dead end at the same time! This was only the beginning of hopes and disappointments. I had already gotten discouraged, obviously not trusting God with this. I put it off again.

In January, 1992, I decided to go for it again, and trusted God would help me find my mom. I started by calling all the Jenkins' in the phone book. I wanted to reach that family I met at work. I reached that same gentleman and he handed me over to his sister. She is a wonderful lady. She gave me my mother's maiden name, her mother's name and her first husband's name! She also gave me the name of my mom's first daughter. This meant I wasn't her first born and that I had a real sister somewhere! Boy was I getting excited! I sure had a lot of questions. The big one was, is this really my mother and was I on the right path? No one in the Jenkins family knew where my birth mom would be now. So I was still at another dead end. I kept praying.

February 15, 1992 I joined an organization called "Palm." Palm stands for "parents and adoptees liberated movement." I met and heard birth mothers and adoptees speak. Some had been searching for years. Some found their loved one and there were both happy and sad reunions. Some even refused reunions! Talk about causing mixed emotions for me. I actually felt fear rising inside me. Could I handle another rejection in my life? I knew God was in control and I felt compelled to go on. I was given a number for a search registry and called. An· other dead-end. I was told to check the automobile registry. They said she must have changed her name, is out of the state, or is no longer driving. Another dead-end.

On February 24 I heard from Aunt Ruth again (birth mom's sister in-law from first marriage.) She was able to give me the names of my mother's two sisters, Evelyn and Barbara Carol. My given name at birth being Carol Evelyn, I wondered, "Could not just be a coincidence that I might be named after my two aunts and my mom?" Remember that my name was not changed at my adoption. I began to pray even more for God's direction. I really felt I was on the right track for the right person.

In March I was unable to find my adoption decree: the only proof I had of my birth mother and that I was adopted! I sent to family court for a copy, and did not hear from them for a month! In April I called them. I had mailed the letter to the wrong address! I sent another one. I received a letter from family court staying that there were no such papers filed through them! I must have been adopted through the probate court. So frustrating! Yet prayerfully I pursued. In the meantime, my daughter, Debbi, found my original paper at her Dad's house. God is so good! So many dead-ends though. Where do I go from here? I just knew God knew where my mom was. I felt that by His Holy Spirit He could guide me to her and my family. My fervent prayer was: "Lord, show me the way to find my mom, if it be Thy will and for Your glory. I believe, in Jesus Name, you are able to lead me to her; and Lord, if possible, perform a miracle and let me find her for Mother's Day, 1992. Thank you, Lord. Amen."

Watch how God unfolded His miracle for me. On May 4th, I met an investigator in the office where I worked. He, too was adopted and had attempted a search, but stopped. He suggested I locate all my adoption papers. This is really an impossible task because all adoption records in the 1940s are permanently sealed. Was it just a coincidence that I met this nice gentleman or God's perfect plan? God knows who we need at just the right time. First I decided to call all the names in the phone book that were my mom's maiden name. My first call was a sweet, elderly lady. She was my mom's aunt by marriage. Boy, was I getting excited. She gave me the name and phone number of her daughter. She felt her daughter would remember things better than she did. I called right away and was given mom's second husband's name. I was also told Mom had another son and daughter. That meant I had another sister and brother somewhere, both younger than me! Then I was informed that she had a third husband who died; and also married a fourth time. She also knew Mom's last known marriage name!

Later I was informed that Mom's sister Evelyn was in a nursing home with Alzheimer's and would not be able to help me. I did visit her though. I wasn't sure if she understood me. She held my hand tight like she knew me and wouldn't let go. The nurse said she never acted that way with anyone else. I felt God was using her in some way to keep me going . . . that I was on the right track.

Another relative phoned me to let me know I had a cousin Norman who could probably help me locate my mom. Everyone in the Jenkins family was always calling me to try and help in some way. Cousin Norman was Aunt Evelyn's son and Mom's nephew. When given his address I realized he lived in the same mobile park where I lived! It is a small world, especially in Rhode Island!

On May 7, 1992, I found out that my cousin's phone number was unpublished. I called the park landlord to see if he could give it to me or at least call them to have them call me. She gave me the phone number and the lot number their home was on. I went right over there. They were not home! I left a note stating I thought I might be his cousin. I would give details if he'd call me. I left my phone number and name. He called that evening and invited me to visit with him and his lovely wife, Sue. He listened to me attentively as I told my story of the past eight month search. Giving attention to every detail. Guess he wanted to be sure too. All of a sudden he said, "okay, I've heard enough. You are definitely my cousin. I knew you existed but never dreamed this would ever happen."

He got up and left the room. He came back with picture albums! We looked through them for quite awhile. We agreed there definitely was a distinct family resemblance. Then he told me he knew where my mom, sister and brother lived! I think my heart wanted to pound out of my chest at this point! I was both excited and scared. What I actually prayed for was really happening! Should I be surprised with the great God I serve in control? I just wish I could always be as faithful to Him as He is to me.

My mom and sister were living in Rochester, New York. My brother was right here in Rhode Island. That was not all; he also had their phone numbers! I was shaking and crying by now. My cousin took me in his arms to console me. This was only the beginning of another journey in my life.

My cousin Norman and I decided it would be better for him to call my sister with all this news. We didn't even know if she was ever told I existed! We felt she could talk with Mom personally instead of hearing it over the phone. He said Mom had been very ill a few times. He wasn't sure how she was now. I left my phone number with Norman to give to my sister if she wanted it. I knew it was out of my hands.

I prayed some more, trusting God with this whole situation. Also still hoping I found the right person! How could I be positively sure? Questions went through my mind. Will she deny having me? Maybe she won't remember or won't want to see me. I felt I needed and wanted more proof. I remember I needed to try to get more adoption papers if possible. I found out how to reach probate court. I had to call every city and town in Rhode Island! Not that many cities, right? Smallest state in 'the Union! I finally found my records in Cranston. I gave the clerk my information and she said for me to wait while she went to check. I was actually shaking. I almost knew she was going to come back and say the records were sealed!

A quick prayer came from my lips, "Lord, I need another miracle." Another lady came to the phone. She said she had my folder in her hands. There were many papers in it. I asked her if she could give me some information from them. She suggested I get down there to see what I needed. I couldn't believe my ears, but I did not dare question her. Was this lady an angel? If she wasn't, she was to me! I went right down there.

No one knew what I was talking about when I got there! I did not know what to do. I knew I didn't dream it all, I really spoke with someone in that office!

I started to walk out the door disappointed, when this short lady appeared behind the counter. She asked if she could help me. I told her my name and she said for me to wait a minute. She had them ready for me. My heart was pounding again! She came back and handed me the whole folder! She said to let her know if I wanted anything copied. I was excited, yet shaking. I hoped I wasn't doing something illegal! No one was stopping me.

There were other people all over that office. Two papers had my mother's maiden name on them and her signature. This was proof that it was my birth mom I had found. I had found my birth mom in time for Mother's Day, 1992, just as I prayed I would! The lady gave me the copies I needed. I told her how happy she had made me. She said she could tell by the look on my face, and that she was glad she could be of help at a special time like this. Do you know I looked for that nice short lady at the courthouse later to thank her and share all that happened? I even knew her name was Anna. No one knew her! They said she might have been filling in that day. I'd like to think she was one of God's messengers. Strange, but miraculous!

Meanwhile, in New York, my younger sister was notified. I later found out she was both skeptical and excited. She couldn't understand why Mom never told her she had a sister. She knew about our older sister and that her dad's family raised her. She also wondered if I had proof. What if Mom denied it or doesn't want to remember! She had the same questions I had. She felt if she had a sister who wants to know her family, then she wanted to know me. That's how she approached our

Mom. I found out later that they all knew Jesus Christ as their personal Lord and Savior. My sister was praying all the way to Mom's apartment. She had also called her daughters and they were very happy and excited.

Well, she told Mom. They talked and then she called me! She said, "Is this my long lost sister?" My heart leaped! She continued, "Mom says she doesn't remember any details, but yes you are her daughter." We were both crying tears of joy by now. I told her I had copies of my adoption papers. She said I really didn't need them, but she'd like to see them. Then I realized she was at "our mother's" apartment, and that Mom wanted to speak to me too.

I will never forget the first time I spoke with my birth mom. She sounded very warm and loving. She told me to come see her as soon as possible, she was very anxious to see me! I was just about off the ground with excitement by then! I told my sister I had partially packed already. If God answered my prayer to find my mom, I was going to see her on Mother's Day, 1992! They both said, "come along." My sister gave me directions. It would be a six-hour trip. I began thinking about a friend, who would be free to go with me, so I wouldn't have to ride alone. I called Eleanor and she was thrilled to go with me and be a part of such a happy reunion.

We arrived at a corner store near Mom's apartment where my sister said she'd meet us. We left our cars, looked at each other, and then embraced. It was like two sisters who hadn't s 'en one another in a long time. It was so wonderful . . . so real! Her youngest daughter Joy, my niece, was in the car. I was so happy to meet her. I gave her a big hug and told her how blessed I was 'to find my family. Then I followed my sister to Mom's apartment. We had both thought to bring family picture albums. As I entered the apartment, I quickly dropped the books anxious to go to Mom as I spotted her in her chair. One look and Mom put her arms out to me as you would a child. I ran to her chair and knelt by her. I almost felt like a small child again in her arms. We held each other for several minutes, crying with joy, realizing how alive the bond was between us. God had brought Mom through several serious illnesses. We believe he spared her life so mother and daughter could be reunited after 49 years.

That Mother's day weekend is a time I will never forget. Words cannot express what I felt in my heart when I realized I had found my whole family. My daughter, Debbi was the only one I had time to tell about finding Mom and my sister, before I left that weekend. She was thrilled and excited; and so were my grandchildren, Jenni and Jeff. My sister spoke with our brother; he's the quiet, shy one in the family so I found out. He was surprised to hear he had another sister. I looked forward to meeting him and sister number one when I got back to Rhode Island.

As soon as I got home I called my son, Dave, in Florida. He was so happy for me! We talked for over an hour. I thank God for filling many voids in my life and for this wonderful miracle he performed. Giving me family . . . the second time around!

June 1992. I want to share about my oldest sister, Joanie. I spoke with her Aunt Ruth again. I asked if she thought my sister would like to meet me. Here again I may be facing rejection, yet I was excited. She said she'd call and ask her. Joanie said yes! I later found out she has a "big family" and really didn't need an addition to it, but here I was! We had a bit in common since we were the two daughters Mom had to give up for different reasons. Her Dad's mom raised Joanie. She knew what it was like to have biological kinfolk. She had reservations about meeting me. Said her family was big enough. blame her. After all I was a complete stranger. Yet, if I was really her sister, she was not about to reject me. Thank God for that! I was so happy to get to know her. I was really blessed because later I got to meet all my new nephews and nieces and great nephews and nieces! Boy did my family grow fast! Joanie is a real encouragement to me. As is her daughter Robyn, who is just like her mom, very caring and loveable. Joanie became the typical "big sister" I always wished I had. I love her clearly and thank God she is my sister. I love you and your family very much, Joanie.

I eventually got to meet my brother also. It took Mom coming to Rhode Island for a visit and staying with me, to get him to come meet me. I felt a wonderful closeness with him too. He sure did act like a kid brother . . . teasing me right from the start. I loved it! I love you, Rich. He was divorced; but I got to meet and know my sister in-law, Deb. I grew to love her dearly along with my two nieces and nephew, Marsha, Patty and David. Can you believe it! My only brother and we both named our only sons, David!

After almost a year of traveling to New York to visit Mom and writing faithfully, Mom decided she wanted to move back to Rhode Island. We got to see each other a lot then. We made a lot of wonderful memories. We also made a point to get together as often as possible with Mom's new granddaughter and great grandchildren, my family.

God gave me another year with Mom before she took very ill again. It was time for her to leave the hospital and so she asked to go back to New York. She knew she was too sick to live alone anymore. My brother and I were alone, so we had to work and were unable to care for her in our homes. My sister, brother and I are all nurses, something Mom said she always wanted to be. My sister ran a nursing care agency, so she could arrange for Mom to have the care she needed whenever Sis couldn't be home. My brother flew Mom back to New York. She was there for about a week when Rich and I were called. My sister said she didn't think Mom would make it through the night. We tried to get there in time, but didn't make it. My sister even tried to ask Mom who my dad was, but Mom took that information to heaven with her. It's okay. Somehow I am satisfied with all the "family" God has blessed me with. "I love you so much, Mom. Thank you for choosing to let me live." I told her that when I met her. I think about my life every time I hear about the abortion issue. I wonder and grieve about those babies who would love to live. They can't make the choice. Their mother has to make it for them. God's will is to give us life. I don't feel anyone on earth has the right to choose if a baby should have the right to life or not. If you don't want the child you're bearing, there are other options. There are many that for some reason are not naturally blessed with children. That child that would have been aborted could live a full life with a family who wants a child to love.

CHAPTER X

Choices Can Bring Bondage or Freedom

I know I've mentioned my tendency to love people too much. I want to come back to that again. Through the years, many would say that I beamed with the love of God. They could feel His love flow through me to them. Yet the enemy would often want to warp that love, distort it, and confuse it. Now I see as I look back, and thank God for His keeping Power. I see how the voids, hurts, disappointments, neglects and who knows what else can cause us to make wrong choices. Many things, circumstances in life, can make us vulnerable to the devil's temptations and traps.

This flesh we are made of is weak. That is why it is so important to continue to be strengthened spiritually. Strengthened by prayer, daily bible reading, fellowship and assembling together with other Christians of like-precious faith. It is possible at any time in our life to be overtaken unawares, so we must always set a watch on our hearts. It doesn't matter how long we have been walking with God. "Be sober, be vigilant; because your adversary the devil as a roaring lion walking about, seeking whom he may devour." (1Peter 5:8) The devil wants to destroy us, not only spiritually, but also physically. He wants us to love too much, which is possible . . . as I will explain further in my story. He wants us to be compulsive or addictive with anything and everything. God says, everything in moderation. Only God, through the power of His Holy Spirit living within us can help us keep things in proper perspective and in moderation. He needs to be first in our lives, and then He can help us stay in control.

Let me explain what happened to me next and how I backslid from walking with God. It is difficult to realize today how I could have ever left my first love, Jesus, but I did. This is why I feel it is so important to share this with others. I was the one who chose to make other things number one in my life, instead of God. When this happened the things of God also faded in importance to me. It was something I never thought would or could happen. I was saved 23 years.

After losing my second husband, I was devastated. I got to a place where I was no longer content. I became restless living up north. The winter came; this was the second winter alone. It was a terrible winter. I became cold, dismayed and lonely. That was the winter I moved to Florida. My son had a home there and said he'd be thrilled for me to stay with him as long as I needed or wanted to. As I said before, I am not one to depend on my children for long. Being a nurse, I was confident that God would help me find employment. At that point in my life, I was feeling desperate for change. I couldn't take one more winter alone in Rhode Island! I have no doubt; it was God's will for me to move to Florida. When I made my decision, I felt that peace only He can give come over me. Besides, three days later provisions were made to take care of the trailer I lived in. This meant I could plan to move when I was ready; there was nothing stopping me.

I moved to Florida. I lived with my son, Dave, for a couple of months. It took me that long to look for employment. Sometime later, I made another big change which helped me cope with the loss of my husband. Since I hadn't carried his name very long, I decided to go back to my maiden name, Lang. I also changed my name from Carol to Lynnie, which was part of my middle name and part of my birth mom's name.

I now carried the names from my two families. First name Lynnie, from birth mom's name; last name, Lang from adopted family name. Shortly after this was all legalized, while working for a temporary nursing service, I met a fellow employee Linda, who soon became a great friend. Through her influence I was introduced to the personnel director of Orange County Corrections, the Orlando county jail. I was hired and put on their nursing staff. Once I got settled in work, I moved into my own apartment. Some choices, as I said before, help and some hinder our lives. This one was a tremendous help.

Some time passed and I found myself attending different churches. Couldn't seem to get planted in a church body. Believe me, church hopping is very unhealthy spiritually. We need to be rooted with a church body, so we can watch and pray for each other. I missed my church family at Frenchtown Baptist Church in Rhode Island very much.

There's safety in being part of the body of Christ. We watch out for one another's souls. We build one another up in the faith. Assembling together builds strength in God to fight the hard times life offers. Most important God, through Christ, is the center of all we do. Without Jesus Christ as the center of our lives we are definitely putting something else in the center. Even though I knew Jesus was my Savior and the Lord of my life, it didn't mean I always allowed Him to be the center of all I did. Here is where the danger lies in falling into Satan's deceptions. I gradually moved from my total commitment to God to being more concerned about myself. Loneliness, boredom and depression during or after life's crisis and transitional periods (big changes) can make us very vulnerable.

Again I began searching for a church home. I was desperate for Christian fellowship. I became discouraged, attending some church every week, yet not fitting in. I needed friends and wasn't making any. I felt myself sinking, yet didn't realize that spiritually I was drained. I read God's Word, but not like I used to. I had no one to reach out to and have pray for me. No church I would attend on Sunday, would I really become a part of. So again, I was on the outside looking in. This is a dangerous place to be spiritually. Just attending a church and reading your Bible doesn't equip a Christian for life's turns in the road.

I became centered on self and self's need s and wants. My life was no longer centered on God as it had been for 23 years. I wasn't even aware of the wilderness journey I was heading into. Being a people oriented type of person; I missed my friends up north terribly. I made the mistake of forgetting I had a best friend who is always with me and never forsakes me, Jesus. Yet, as much as we say we love God and desire His will, we are not infallible. Our minds can become the devil's playground; if they are not renewed daily by the Word of God and prayer, (Communicating with God). We become prey to Satan's lies and deception, if we desire only to please ourselves.

I was not content and felt very alone. My son was here, but I knew he has his own life to live. He was always there *if* I needed him as we visited regularly. It is not like having a friend or friends you can call and talk with and fellowship with. I am definitely not sure if I was praying for God's will at this point, probably not. I wanted friends and I was desperately lonely! After a while I was at work and met a fellow worker. She was younger than I was, more my daughter's age. We hit it off rather quickly. She lived with her mom. Soon I had two new friends and was so thankful. I got what I asked for. I believe special people are put in our lives for God's purpose. He never stops teaching us, but sometimes He has to wait till we're ready to learn. I can't believe it took me so long to realize what He wanted me learn!

For some reason I wasn't finding a life for myself. It did seem my life, unaware to me at the time, always centered on the people I was with. God has always been in my life, since I committed my life to Him in 1970. Yet I have always felt I needed someone to belong to. Adopted kids, at least this adopted kid, start off knowing they were rejected at birth. They seem to go through life trying to belong, or at least be accepted and not rejected. People in life seem to disappoint you, but not on purpose. Their life goes on and we find ourselves left behind, when we lean on a person instead of God. Let me go on and explain. Time went by and we had a wonderful relationship. My friend and I had many good times together. Later she bought a home and invited me to move with her and share expenses.

This was when my "wilderness" journey really began. I gradually became more and more emotionally dependent on my friend. I began to believe the lies Satan was feeding my mind instead of the truths of God. Satan is the author of confusion and deception. He is the greatest liar. Just as Eve believed His lie, we too can fall into his deception and believe His lies.

What happened was a beautiful relationship centered in God became two people totally centering their lives on each other. I became a people pleaser instead of always desiring to please God as I did most of my life. I became a lover of pleasure instead of a lover of the things of God. I kept God to one side in my life. Our lives became so closely enmeshed that I could' not imagine us ever being apart. Eventually my life, even my identity, was lost in hers. I got to a place; I was planning nothing without consulting her first. We had friends, but rarely got together with them separately. A wonderful friendship had become the worst bondage I had ever experienced in my life! I had realized how far away from God I had gotten. I wasn't doing anything I used to do to keep me in tune with God. Totally depending on her to make all my decisions, I allowed her to control everything in my life including my finances. I was barely responsible for anything in my life any more!

My friend and I went on vacation up north to visit folks in Rhode Island and Massachusetts. My daughter, Debbi had noticed I let my friend make all the decisions. She said to herself, "It seems like my mom can't do anything on her own anymore; she allows her friend to tell her what to do and when to do it." She became very concerned, so she talked with me later. Even then, I was not truly aware. We were leaving and I was saying goodbye to my daughter. She told me she would be praying for me; that it troubled her to see me allow someone to run my life.

Her words never left me after we got home. God used my daughter, Debbi's love and prayers to begin to set me free. Finally I realized I had no life of my own. I was so much in darkness; I could no longer see the light! "Lord, I need You," I cried. "I no longer know where I am or even who I am! Please help me find my way back to You·." I recommitted my life to Jesus Christ, and asked God to take complete control.

Very soon, I got in contact with a wonderful counselor. I was very comfortable talking with her. I came to decisions I knew God was telling me to make. I also felt He would give me the strength to carry them through. I knew there would be some consequences to face. I would never intentionally want to hurt anyone, but I knew the decision I was about to make would definitely hurt my friend.

Somehow I knew she would not understand that it was best for both of us to separate. It was time for me to go out on my own again. I needed to find myself, and get back to my place in God where I belong. I walked out of her home and into God's arms and grace completely.

He has been letting me experience His presence like never before. In my own home I never felt alone, He was always present. I talk with Him all the time. Jesus is truly my best friend once again. I can truly sing one of my favorite songs; *"Jesus is the Best Friend I Ever Had." He has done me nothing but good, takes away the bad. He picks me up when I'm down; cheers me when I'm sad. Jesus is the best friend I ever had.* I have also come to realize that I need to guard and treasure my place with God. If I don't I can slip and fall away from Him again.

It is so important to choose our friends carefully and wisely. When we have committed our lives to Christ, there is a danger in choosing to be close to those who do not desire the same faith. God will never turn from me, I can choose to turn from Him at any time, even for a season. He gave us a free will to choose to serve and please Him with our lives or not. It is sad to see folks, who choose to serve Satan, sin and self and stay in the darkness of this world, turn from you as they have Jesus.

Jesus is the light of truth, which makes those rejecting the light uncomfortable when in the presence of God's people. It saddens me to see folks choose to live without the peace of God in their hearts. He waits so patiently for us. Calling to us to come to Him, yet we do not listen or want to hear Him. He has such a better life for us to live. All we have to say is yes to Him.

He longs to fulfill His purpose for your life.

I pray that my experience will be an inspiration and encouragement to others that may have lost their way. Turn to Jesus, He is waiting for you with open arms to receive you, forgive you, and help you to go on. He will even heal the hurts of your past. What a great God we serve. He is able to deliver you from the snares of the devil. Just let go and let God have His way. He loves you and only wants His best for you. People will let you down, but God is always faithful. My counselor told me I didn't need to see her any longer. She was amazed at my progress and how God had set me free. She could see I was totally trusting God with my life. He was in control and I was at peace with my soul. I still stayed in touch with another counselor in a Christian support group called Eleutheros, in Orlando.

Eleutheros means freedom from bondage. Most often when we come out of broken relationships, we are broken people. The support of Christians who have "been there" helps tremendously. They can encourage us when we see how God has put back the pieces of their lives and made them whole again. Why did God allow all this? Life is a challenge, but is filled with opportunities for God to work in and through us.

We gain understanding and wisdom through every challenge when we seek and desire it. Wisdom is all knowledge and understanding finally being able to be used for God's glory. Do we consciously seek wisdom in every situation and from past mistakes? We need always to seek God when making choices, not just do what we think will make us happy. Now I see . . . this is exactly what I did. Good counseling and spiritual support can help us learn and grow through all adversities in life.

CHAPTER XI

New Beginnings, New Challenges

I began to search for a church. This time I meant business with *God:* I asked Him for a church that was alive with His Spirit. Where He was moving in and through His people, healing and changing lives. It is exciting to be moving forward with God. If I'm not going forward, it means I am either standing still or going backwards. I do not want to be doing either. I now look forward to the plans God has for me. He desires only to enrich my life. Well, He sure led me to a great church. Being from Rhode Island, I am not use to big churches. I feel lost in them. Again God is always willing to teach us new things.

He did lead me to a big church. I could feel God's presence as soon as I entered the church. I recognized the happy faces on God's people. I felt His love from their loving hugs of welcome. That day the pastor opened the altar for prayer. I went forward to publicly recommit my life to Jesus. I thanked God for every experience He had brought me through. They would not only enrich my life in His truth, but that my life may touch others also with that truth.

Pinecastle United Methodist Church in Orlando, Florida became my home church. Because of the size, folks are encouraged to become a part of smaller groups that serve in the church. There are prayer groups and bible studies for all age groups, singles, couples, men and women. It is a very active body of Christ with a heart to reach out to those who need to hear it.! who Jesus really is. If you attend a large church, be sure you're . . . getting involved in smaller groups that can minister to you in a personal way. God is so good, He blessed me with some great friends, a spiritual mom, dad and gram; and my church family who loved and cared for me.

Let me back up again to focus on some rich lessons I've learned. I believe we have choices. We can choose to belong to and serve God or we can reject Him and His will for us. Then we lay prey to Satan's power to rule in our lives. When we choose to serve Satan, his demons work overtime to take control of every area we yield to him and his schemes, driving you and tempting you to do things God never intended for you to do; forcing you to be someone you are really not. Yet you believe his lie. You feel you are who you want to be through more deception. You have chosen to allow Satan to have his way with your life, instead of God!

Now when God is asked to reign supreme in your life, He does so. His Son Jesus Christ, who died for our sins, will become your Lord and Savior only when you ask. God never forces His will on you. He gave you a free will. He desires you to be in His divine will for He knows what is best for you, much better than you know yourself. God comes alive in our lives through His Holy Spirit. Our spirit, which is dead because of sin, becomes spiritually alive by the indwelling of God's Spirit. He gently and gradually molds you into the vessel of honor

He intended you to be. Then and only then are you truly free to be you.

I do want to add one thing here. Yes, sin separates us from God. There is no time that God does not love you. We, God's people, are saved from our sinful past, forgiven, but we are not perfect. If you are a child of God, don't turn your back on the one still trapped in sin. Remember always from where God has brought you. We can still fall back without God's grace and power active in our lives. I have been there and done that! We make the mistake of judging the person instead of the sin they are caught up in. They don't know how to get out of it any more than we did, until someone cared enough to tell us that we could be set free. We are to hate the sin, but we are to love the sinner. "But God commended His love towards us in that, while we were yet sinners, Christ died for us." (Romans 5:8). You may be the only door for that one caught up in sin. You are there and ready to help them know there is a better life awaiting them. God is waiting to lead and guide them into all truth. Believe me, if someone is totally rejecting Christ, they will reject you too. Someone was there to lead you to Jesus, Who is the way, the truth and the life for them too. We need to give everyone the chance to make the choice as we did. Just a little nugget I thought I'd give to my sisters and brothers in Christ. Remember to reach out and touch that one who is lost in sin's trap with the love of God that dwells in you.

Now I will get back to my story. What has God always intended for me to be? His child. He asks for me to be totally dependent on Him. He desires to teach me, direct my path, meet my needs and admonish me when I begin to stray. He wants to because He is a loving Heavenly Father.

I have always felt I needed to conform. What was I conforming to, the image of the god of this world and his evil ways? At one time in my life I even conformed to a religion. Yes, we can become compulsive and dependent on a religion. I thought I had to work for a place with God. I got into bondage with all kinds of rules. Doing all this good stuff for God must make us more holy, so I thought. It was so difficult to try to live a perfect life. We will never be perfect, no matter how hard we try. That is why God knew we needed a Savior and sent His Son.

Sometimes it was difficult for me to realize that I am not under the law, but under grace. The grace of God has set me free. Not free to sin, but free to please God with my life. I don't know how anyone's life can change for the better without God's help. All He wants is for us to desire to turn from our sinful ways. We surrender all to Him. We actually give up. We stop and let go and let God take charge of our lives. What He feels needs changing in us, we will then desire to be changed. It will come naturally as we allow the Holy Spirit to work in and through us.

So much has come to pass since I started writing this book. I would never have imagined all that has transpired. I am so grateful to my God who is faithful to watch over me. My fervent prayer is that I may be faithful to Him for the rest of my life.

There is more I want to encourage you with. Those of you who may have the tendency to let others consume your life . . . there is hope. I had never heard of it before, but this tendency is called Codependency or Emotional Dependency. It took me fifty years to hear those words and learn about it. You can know there are support groups that help you learn to trust God totally. It is unhealthy to always lean on another person for everything. God does make a way for you to be set free from bondage to a person or a substance. Let me go on and explain a little further of my own experiences.

A familiar tone for many of us who have codependent behaviors is to stay stuck in a dead relationship, not knowing how or why we should get out. Yet we seem to get more miserable as time goes on. Oh, what we do with our lives! Is it really what God intended for us? Of course not! Then what is a person to do? It all has to do with choices. Our choices for our lives may not have been God-ordained, yet He uses everything, even our mistakes, to try to bring us into His divine will. We stay in pitfalls until we can't stand it anymore. We may leave and try to start all over again; or we may finally surrender and turn to God. Then and only then He is able to help us. He will pull us up, lead us out and into His divine will for us.

We choose to allow Him to have control of all situations and circumstances in our lives. All relationships cause growing pains. I believe we can learn and grow stronger spiritually from them. It is God's will for us to focus on Him through all relational problems.

I remember a friend telling a story recently. This really happened. There was a dead chicken on the side of the road. He got out of the car to check things out. There was a live chicken hovering next to it with no intention of leaving. He couldn't even make it leave. Isn't that how some of us have been or maybe still are? Stuck in a dead relationship and have no intention of moving or changing things. I don't know what makes us feel like God intended for us to not have our needs met, and to have verbal, emotional and even physical abuse to be a part of our lives! Yet we allow it and we try to tolerate it day in and day out. We feel there is nothing we can do about it, and some feel they even deserve it! This is not God's intention for any relationship.

Whenever these things enter a relationship, we need help. Sometimes it is recommended to detach for a time to allow God to renew you spiritually from the abusive situation and let both parties seek healing and Christian counseling. Getting your lives centered in Christ is your first priority. It is very difficult to reason why we stay locked into a life that makes us s miserable. CHOICES! God has given us choices. Life is made up of choices. We make our choices and when they make us miserable, we won't make the choice to change things. Do we deserve to be punished because we make wrong choices? No, God, in His mercy tells us that when we sin, ask forgiveness, walk away and don't look back. He forgives and forgets. We need to forgive ourselves. With God's help we can get out, get up and get a life.

Leaving the old behind, we can walk in newness of life. God only can restore what He chooses to restore, you must choose what will bring you back to reality. This can happen often in a lifetime, and for many reasons, and in different types of relationships. It is okay; just keep moving forward in God and closer to God. Look back only to learn and receive the good that has come out of the experiences life has brought us through. Do not dwell on or fret on the negative, but go forth with a positive outlook, looking forward to what God has prepared for us around the next bend in our life. When we make choices to close a door behind us, it allows God to open other doors of opportunity for His will to be done.

Seek God's will and trust Him. Know that even if you go your own way at times, you will have the circumstances to suffer. God is always there, waiting and wanting you to seek Him first. He loves you and forgives you. He is a very patient Father. Ready to help us turn our lives around and decide to do things His way instead of ours. I've experienced His blessings awaiting me to show me, "This is the way, walk ye in it." (Isaiah 30:21) He alone knows what is best for us. I know I have said some things before, but they are worth repeating. We need to seek His guidance and protection when making all decisions. The Holy Spirit will help us discern what is good and what is not. The way I have experienced guidance and protection from God is through prayer and His Word.

Let me share another situation I got myself into recently. It is, February now. I started dating again. I was seeing two very nice gentlemen. I was also in touch with an old friend. The attention was nice and I realized how much I had missed male companionship. I also noticed and felt myself very vulnerable and insecure about my choices. I spoke with each of them about my commitment to God. Letting them know. He is and always will be number one in my life. I longed to please Him in all that I do.

Informing them that I wanted nothing more than a friendship, I asked them how they felt about Jesus. That is a sure way to discover where your friend's relationship with God is. They soon stopped calling me. I now desire to date only those of like precious faith, those who also want the fullness of God's grace in their life. It is even okay now if there isn't a special someone in my life. Jesus is the best friend I ever had, still is and always will be.

It seems like I am waiting on God in so many areas of my life right now. I can feel His presence in my home. I never feel alone anymore. I know He cares for me and is watching over me. I have such a peace as I am learning to wait and lean on Him. Waiting for Him to bring my life together as He planned it to be. Usually I am anxious when I don't know what is ahead for me. I usually map things out for myself, that is when I am in control. I was always trying to figure out how I was going to make things go my way! Resting in the arms of God is just that, resting, watching Him unfold each new day for me. He desires to meet my needs and direct my path, continually showing me His love. He even puts me with the people I need to be with to learn and grow spiritually. Do you know God is working His purpose for you with everyone you are with each day of your life? People will encourage, build you up in the faith and will influence a closer walk with God for you. They will if they know and love God for themselves that is. Those who don't, offer other alternatives for your life. If you ·can't trust God when rough times come, then who or what will you trust to get you through? Life in this world is not easy, rough times are guaranteed in a world of darkness. People will let you down, but God is always faithful. He is always there for you.

I think I mentioned God giving me a new spiritual mom and dad, Joan and Bill. They are so precious. I love them so much! God truly knows how to fill the voids in our lives if we let, Him. We, in our human nature, try to fill the hurts, losses and disappointments with the things of this world. Yes, we need people, but only the love of Jesus can truly fill all your needs, as He has mine. He can only fill you as you empty yourself of your old nature. Little by little as He makes known to you what is not pleasing to Him, you will desire to give it over to H!m; and He will help you do it. He loves you and wants to fill your spiritual being to overflowing with His divine nature. Your life being lost in God's, you can be confident of His will in your life being fulfilled.

CHAPTER XII

Commitments Require Right Choices

March. Another month has gone by. What a glorious month it has been. I love the church I am attending now. I feel so loved and accepted. I had visited several churches in the area. Do you know you really need a church body, "God's people," who you fit in with, and who will encourage your spiritual growth? God knows what we need. He gave me a real peace inside when I was where He wanted me to be. Our church has many choices of Sunday school classes, prayer meeting groups and bible study groups. Many committed, dedicated Christians conduct activities of all kinds for a variety of ages and time schedules. Sometimes it takes patience and perseverance to find where you need to be. I was determined and prayerful because I wanted to be where God wanted me to be.

I wanted so much to touch the hearts of those lost in sin and see God draw them to Himself. The only way we can become useful to God is to be available to Him. First to allow Him to mold us, into who He wants us to be, useful, willing vessels, fit for the Master's use. When we ask Him into our lives, He does what we ask. By His Holy Spirit, He fills our hearts to overflow out to others. It is so exciting to be a servant of the Lord. I have truly been blessed to be able to attend Sunday worship service, a mid-week prayer meeting and a bible study. I work evenings, 2:30-10:30p.m. so it was great to have a variety of meetings to choose from.

It is wonderful to gather together with others to feed on God's Word and pray for one another and our loved ones. I pray I can be prepared to serve wherever He leads me. I am so happy to be back in God's will again. "Now I see" it is very easy to slip away; and get caught up in the things of this world. We need to always be on guard for Satan, the enemy of our souls. He is robbing many beautiful people from the blessings and freedom they can have in Jesus Christ. I know I robbed myself for a time! God never forces us to follow Him. We must be careful not to become prey to the devil. He comes into a life as an angel of light with his cunning craftiness. He will persuade you to give in to his schemes, which only lead to darkness and destruction. We need good strong Christian fellowship, accountability, the study of God's Word and a place to worship Him where you feel His presence.

Your church home needs to be a place where you can receive prayer and spiritual encouragement. All this is very necessary for your spiritual maturity. If we get away from our dedication to our higher power, God, then we dedicate ourselves to other things. These other things are usually contrary to God's will. This is when Satan is controlling what we do. How do I know? I know from experience. It's our best teacher. Spiritual elders, those who have "been there," are a big help. Listen to those who appear to have received such wisdom.

Here is another nugget to help understand the forces of evil in this world. Satan always "forces" us to do what he wants us to do. He even learns our weak areas from our past experiences. He has many methods of force: coaxing, tempting, persuading, inducing, pressuring, threatening, intimidating, influencing, compelling through pressure or necessity, inflicting, imposing, constraining, necessitating, obligating, manipulating and con· trolling. All of which are forms of using others or things to force you into following his destructive ways.

When you choose to allow God to take control of your life, He patiently waits for you to call on Him. Through the redemptive power of His Son, Jesus Christ, the Holy Spirit gently guides you into His truths concerning your life. It is in knowing that He died for you, that you can be set free from the bondage of in and spiritual death. We can come to Him, putting our sin!! Under the blood Jesus shed for us. This is when we desire and are able, with His help, to turn from our wicked ways and follow His way. He is faithful to cleanse our hearts and minds of all uncleanness and will deliver us from evil.

God is so good. I have been experiencing Him touching my life in such real ways. He is meeting my every need 'and fulfilling my desires. Do you know that God knows the desires of our hearts? He knows how to meet our needs better than we do ourselves! Financially it has been very tight since I am living alone now. God has shown me how to be a good steward of my income. I have always given back to the Lord's work what He asks in His Word. I couldn't see how I could now, and still meet my needs. I made the choice to make a check out Sunday for His work, and trust God would show me how to meet my needs.

On Monday I felt led to sit down and redo my budget. I learned a whole new way to manage my finances! All my bills were met on the first of that month, praise God. God is so faithful when we learn to lean on Him; trusting Him with all the details of our lives. The trying of our faith works patience. The things of this world are tempting. When we desire those things God would want us to have: He will freely give us all good things. He withholds nothing from those who love Him. Yet, remember He know what is best for us. He may say no at times. You know then that it is not in your best interest to have it. It could also be the wrong timing. He withholds as any loving father would. A guide that has always helped me is, "if I have doubt, I don't do it." If God doesn't want you to do something, you will feel uneasy about doing it.

When it is His will for you, He gives a peace that passes all understanding. All things work out very smoothly when He is in control. If we do not get that peace, we need to shelve that idea or desire. I wish I could always be sensitive to that. Often my human nature likes to control every situation. I even go ahead of God and do it my way many times. I am learning to wait for His direction, and sometimes it means waiting till the last minute. It does take faith. God is always faithful to provide the answer or the need though. He has never failed to come through for me.

With God's help, my desire is to continue on the path He has prepared for me. I am excited to see what lies ahead. I want to be an example of all God can and will do in someone's life when we allow Him to lead and guide.

CHAPTER XIII

Right Choices Bring Blessings

My nursing position at the jail became too stressful for me, so I decided to retire from the medical profession altogether and take another position within Orange County Corrections. This was another choice that was for my good. I took training to become an officer and work at a control desk now. I controlled the coming and going on inside by closed circuit monitors and two-way radios, plus other interesting duties. I love my job and the staff I worked with. God had also given me the opportunity to be on staff at my church as nursery coordinator, coordinating the nursery volunteers for Sunday services. He just never stops blessing me, and showing me how I can work for Him, and meet my needs too!

Soon after this, I was blessed again. I was able to purchase my own mobile home and a brand new car! I wasn't even thinking along those lines, but the opportunities presented themselves. Financially both changes helped me. I was content with what I had, but not happy. God does know the desires of our hearts and our needs better than we do ourselves. I was uncomfortable living in the area I felt I could afford to live in till I got on my feet financially. I had a friend who was in the same position I was in. Living alone in an uncomfortable area only because she could not afford better. Since I had been so blessed with a home with two bedrooms, I offered to share my home with her. This helped us both financially. then my care blessing happened. I desired a smaller, more economical one, but didn't think I could afford one. God's timing is always best. He knows when and how to work all things together for good to them that love Him and to them called according to His purpose; one of God's promises found in Romans 8:28. What excitement there is when you experience God's provision! Resting in His care brings true contentment.

Another year passed and I felt that I was at another crossroad in my life again. I felt a tugging in my heart to strive to get out of debt completely. I adjusted my budget to pay off things more quickly. I still felt a heaviness in having a mortgage and a car payment. Yet God had opened the door for these things last year. I waited as I usually do for God's intervention in my decisions. I mentioned to a friend at work that I was thinking about selling my mobile home. She asked where I was planning to live. I really didn't know at the time, just felt it was time to sell. She said that she was sure that John, her husband, would want to buy it when he heard. I was shocked and also a bit apprehensive, but we went forward with the plans.

My mobile home was sold and I began to pray for God's direction as to where I was to live. Meanwhile, I had been ministering with gospel songs and bible study at new home ministry opened through my church in Pinecastle. This home was opened to give women in recovery from addictions a Christian home environment. Within a week of the sale of my home I got a phone call.

It was someone who had an addiction problem looking for somewhere to go for help.

I called the church, knowing we had a shelter for women recovering from addictions. The person I contacted was my friend, Melva, who was on the advisory board for the home. She informed me that they were unable to take anyone because they no longer had a director for the women/s home. She had quit. Immediately a concern and a passion rose up in side me. I wanted to help and asked if there was anything I could do. Where would these women go, back to the streets? This can't happen; God doesn't want this! She asked if I were the least bit interested in taking on this ministry, she knew me and felt I could handle the position. Being a nurse would be very helpful when a woman was detoxing, she said. I agreed with her. All I could say was, yes if that is what God would have me do, I was wiling to step out in faith. She asked me to write a spiritual resume and they would bring it before the board. That evening, with the help of the Holy Spirit, I wrote one out to let them know my personal spiritual experiences, training as a Christian Counselor, my nursing education and prior work. I faxed it to them right away. Next day they asked me if I would consider moving into the home, Living Water Ministry, to direct it. I informed her that I needed to take the proper steps to leave my job at the jail. My job had been notified of the changes that may take place in my life, but how soon, we were not sure. Her it was, the big step. I went into my supervisor and told her I was definitely leaving and asked how soon she could let me go. She checked her books, realizing I had a lot of vacation and sick time saved up, that she could use that time for my two week notice. I could leave immediately! I was amazed, but not surprised, because I know that when God had a plan, He works it all out in His time.

I called the church immediately to inform them of the good news. The following weekend the men from the home ministry for men, Foundation for Life, moved me into the ministry home, and I took the position of new director of Living Water Ministry for Women. I served there for a year. Another experience God had planned for me.

Folks, if you are struggling with a relationship, or with emotional problems that are affecting your relationships, I hope this will encourage you. Relationships of any kind, even friendships, are to be chosen wisely. Healthy, Christian friends make healthy, Christian friends. So I encourage you today, if there is a particular relationship issue you are having difficulty with, even with husband or children, Jesus is the answer. We need only to look at ourselves, because we cannot change that other person. God answers prayer, we need to search our own hearts. (Psalm 139:23,24) says: "Search me, O God, and know my heart; try me, and know my thoughts; see if there be any wicked way in me, and lead me in the way everlasting." Prayer is the answer. Prayer changes things and people, if we let God into our lives, as our personal Savior.

CHAPTER XIV

Never Know What
Will Happen Next

Often we are moved back to situations in life, that we thought we left behind. Yet our loving God has a purpose in everything He allows to happen in our lives. It is all for our best, even though we do not realize it all when it is happening.

While working at Living Waters Home for addictive behavior recovery for women, so many times I felt tugs in my heart for my husband. Guilt played a big part in my emotions. Being a nurse, I wanted so much to help and 'fix' people who were suffering and bound; and could not help the one I loved so much in this world. He gave me two beautiful children and our life was happy and content. Things in life seem to want to take us over, so we take our eyes off the only One who gave us the life He intended for us. My hubby and I were in ministry for many years, as we were bringing up our two beautiful children, Debbi and David. Now they were older and living their own lives, and I was living mine. Ken and I had times we totally ignored each other, and times we felt very close. We talked on the phone, in those close times, and now was one of them. I felt a tugging in my heart to be with him. We talked about it. He was still living in Rhode Island, next door to his parents, and I was in Florida. I prayed and the feelings would not leave, got stronger, and I eventually moved back to

Rhode Island. We were reunited once again, and were very happy. He was determined in his heart to work on totally getting off the pain medication he was hooked on. I watched him struggle for so many years! His parents were elderly and not well, yet were able to care for themselves. My dad in law had Dementia, and my mom in law had a bad heart. Not a good combination to be taking care of each other. Eventually we put an intercom system from their home to ours. We were always in touch, in case they needed us. I remember the many times Dad would go for his usual walks. Mom would time him, and when he wasn't back, she'd call to me, and off I went to find him. He always followed the same path, went so far and turned around. I'd find him chatting with a friend on the side of the road, pick him up and bring him home. Such fond memories of a beautiful couple. Also, Mom would hear Ken, not being very nice to me on occasion, and would yell through the intercom to not treat me as he was. He would quickly go to his room, as a child scolded by his mother! He had forgotten about the intercom, it was very sad and difficult to see him behave that way. Nothing and no one seems to be able to calm the addictive behavior, only God, and only when the person wants His help. I believe this is how God taught me to pray fervently and consistently. I would go into prayer with every situation that confronted me.

As I said, Ken's parents were not well. Both knew Jesus as their Savior, praise God. Mom died first, and I remember coming home from the hospital and having to explain this to a man who may not understand where his wife has gone! I showed him her picture, and asked, "who is this, Dad"? He said, "My Evie". I told him as simply as I could, and he responded to me, "Well I have to go with her." I explained to him that, yes He would, when God calls him home, they would be together again. It was only three weeks when Dad's health declined very quickly, and he joined his Evie. This took a big toll on my hubby. A grief counselor came to our home to help us. He wanted no part in speaking with her, yet was polite enough to sit and listen. Never wanting to share his feelings. Our relationship continually became more difficult. I became, once again, very uncomfortable and even unsafe at times. He no longer acted like my husband, and seemed like a totally different man! Not showing these behaviors on the outside, but at home they were continually getting worse. One situation was beyond my bearing. All I could do was run into the bedroom, close the door and pray. For some reason all he did was keep knocking on the door, speaking very angrily to me. I got on the phone with the grief counselor. Hearing me on the phone, quieted him. She advised me to leave the home, while she was on the phone with me. I heard him walk away, and I left our home for the third time in my life! Sad, disappointed, devastated. She told me to zig zag towards the city of Providence; and she would lead me to the shelter there, until I could decide my next step and go somewhere safe.

Wanting to turn to family, yet knowing this was going to hurt them also. Their dad was a wonderful man, and loved dearly. Through all this I learned to love the person and hate what addiction can do to them and family.

Addiction behaviors change a person, turns them into someone you do not recognize at times.

You grow to hate it, because it consumes their whole life. Few understand or truly see how it not only affects the person, but devastatingly affects the ones they live with and those who love him.

I felt guilty so often, because I didn't know what to do to help him. I needed to refocus . . . . on needs I could handle and do something about.

I had turned all my attention on my elderly in-laws, who lived next door needing my help and assistance in their daily needs. I had stayed busy with them. Now they were gone. I can remember the wonderful times we had with Ken's family. His sister, Bev, was always special to me and still is to this day. She seemed to understand the struggle I was in and was always there for me to talk with.

So now, this was another ending in my life, to only bring a new beginning with the God of my salvation at the realm of my ship. Walking with God is an adventure, with all its ups and downs, prayerfully more ups than downs. Each bring the opportunity to draw close to our Lord, and a desire for His leading in our lives. Remember, He uses EVERY circumstance in life as an opportunity for us to learn and see HIS intervention in all that we endeavor to do. "Looking unto Jesus the author and finisher of our faith." (Hebrews 12:2)

I did so, praying all the way. Waiting on God is something we find very difficult to do, especially when things happen so fast. I didn't stay at the shelter long, called my niece, Robyn, and she opened her heart and home to me. Sharing the love of family during another trying time in my life. She encouraged me and that helped me greatly. I had confidence that God had a plan and would show me what I was to do next.

CHAPTER XV

All Things Become New
and Then . . .

That He did . . . . shortly after that, I was heading back to Florida. Of course, everything opened up for me to move back to Saint Cloud Trailer Park to live, got a job quickly, and looked forward for more new things to unfold before me.

We do serve a prayer answering God. God says in His Word, "And to know the love of God, that ye might be filled with all the fulness of God; Who is able to do exceeding abundantly all that we ask or think, according to the power that works in us, unto Him be all honor and glory." (Eph 3:19-21)

We must always accept everything with this on our minds: "For we know that ALL things work together for good to them who love God and are the called according to His purpose." (Romans 8:28) What and who we might have to leave behind us, though very difficult, works for good, as the Scripture says so clearly. Though I certainly didn't see too much of the good at the time, "now I see" God stood beside me all the time. He doesn't take us around, above or below the problems, but through them to yet another phase in our lives.

Being back in Florida was wonderful and a good move for me, as I was getting older, the winters in

New England were rough on me. I settled in, found a wonderful church family, and began to adjust to my surrounding. Seeing old friends again, and making new ones. Content and happy as I served God in my community, in my work and in my church. I felt my life was once again complete. Being in touch with family at a distance, and visiting when it was possible helped a lot. Family is always in your heart no matter how many miles apart we are. All seems to go well for a portion of your life, then unexpectedly, troubles come again . . .

I was at work, and was not feeling well. Being a nurse your mind and thoughts have to stay clear. All of a sudden, I couldn't think right. Not knowing what was happening to me, I called to the other nurse who was on the other wing opposite mine. She came quickly, walked me to the nurses station to sit me down, and take my vital signs. My blood pressure was dangerously high, and I wasn't making much sense by then. She called 911. We both felt this was serious. She was a Christian friend as well as a fellow worker and she began to pray. I became more alert, but very, very weak. After being seen at the hospital, they wanted to keep me for tests. I felt a lot better after being medicated and rested for several hours . . . . I wanted and insisted I go home. I can be pretty stubborn, when it comes to myself and illness. I knew God had brought me through worse than this, and I would be okay. Agreeing to see my doctor the next day and start test to see what caused the problem. I continued to go into these attacks much too often and very shortly my career as a nurse came to a sudden end. One of the attacks had brought on a slight stroke. They were continually changing my medications. It seemed like a guessing game, as to the cause. I was shocked at what my doctor suggested. He said that I needed a special dog to be able to alert me before I went into symptoms. Never heard of this, and I already had a dog. A beautiful little cream color 12 pound poodle. Had trained him to be a therapy dog to visit hospitals and nursing homes with me. We called a school in Orlando, (ABS Service dog school) and they said to bring him there and they would test him. He past the test, and would still train a bit more in order to be certified by their school, as a Medical Service dog He helped me have more confidence to move forward in my life, once again God brought more healing in so many ways. Who knew, a little dog could do so much for someone's life? A true gift from God!

Some years have past, and one summer day when visiting in Massachusetts, Granddaughter Jenni and Hubby Phil, came to talk with me. They had wonderful news that they were going to have a baby. My first great grandchild! How exciting! They also asked me if I would consider moving back to MA and help care for the baby, so Jenni could continue to teach school after her maternity leave. I felt so privileged and honored, I didn't hesitate a moment before saying YES, of course I would love to do that. The plans began to move forward. Jenni found senior housing for me, located between her house and the school, a bit closer to me though. That was perfect, in case she needed to come assist me with anything. I prayed there would be a vacancy when it was time to move. I owned my little trailer in Florida, and my sister decided to buy it from me. So that was taken care of too. What a mighty God we serve! My apartment opened up in plenty of time for the blessed event, and I moved to Massachusetts. Another new adventure for me. Believe me, it was a big step on my part to forsake the Florida weather and move back north. Didn't give it a second thought though, my focus was on my granddaughter's needs and the pleasure I was to have caring for my Great Grandchild. I was very excited, for sure!

I did know my life in Massachusetts was going to be very different from my Florida life. I got myself settled, Family helped me get my home in order and set up for the new baby to come each day to visit Nana and be in my care. I had found a church near home, which is one of my first priorities whenever I move somewhere different.

More adjustments, yet all seemed to go well. Timmy also adjusted to the new surroundings and especially that there was another service dog at church with him! How often does that happen? My dear friend, Sherry, who is blind, and I got to have a very close friendship, with all that we had in common. Having a disability that needed a dog to help us along the way. God's little helpers for sure. No wonder it is said that God made dogs for man's pleasure. We have also found out much more that God put them on this earth for.

The big day came and Naomi Kate was born! The joy of seeing her was beyond my apprehension. I felt so blessed, there are so many who never get to see their GREAT grandchildren. Like her Great Granddaddy. I was sad to think of what he was missing out on. Hating even more the devil's ways of robbing folk from the blessings of God! More reason to tell the good news to those who will listen that Jesus saves and longs for us to surrender all to Him, that He may make us new creatures in Christ. He will not force Himself into your life, or force you do or stop doing anything . . . . you must come freely and desire to become a child of God, that He may change you into His image. Only if you are willing, can He change you and anything that does not please Him. He gave us free will, and lest we follow His will, we will fail and fall short of the glory of God.

The school year went well, and continued into the next school year. My heart was thrilled each day as Jenni brought my GG Naomi to me. We developed a close bond, which I still see with us today. Even though I am back in Florida, we share a special love between us, and can feel it especially when I return for visits each summer. Her mom always made sure to talk about me, so she wouldn't forget me.

My family is very close, maybe not in miles, but in our hearts. I am so grateful for that.

CHAPTER XVI

Life Is An Adventure in Learning

The first year of caring for my Great granddaughter, Naomi, was wonderful and went so well.

Being an infant she wasn't a strain on me at all. I felt I was doing okay, though tired at the end of the week. We enjoyed the summer and had lots of fun together as families do. Then it was buckling down time to get ready for another school year. Me, taking care of a toddler now. She was so much fun. We could go outside and play on nice days, and take walks together. I enjoyed her so, and made it through half the year than began to feel weaker than I liked at times, but ignored it.

One evening, I was signaled by Timmy, took my medication, and waited with him on my lap, monitoring me. I suddenly got severe pain in my back, and felt shortness of breath. I called 911 immediately. Another trip to the hospital . . . . it had been so long . . . . why now, I asked myself. Very disappointed, the doctor informed me that my heart was extremely overworked and that I would have to slow down a lot, to help it strengthen. I mentioned I was caring for my little one, he said definitely cannot continue. I was devastated! How was I ever going to be able to tell my granddaughter, I could no longer care for Naomi?! The ache in my heart was more difficult to bear than the pain I had in my chest and back.

How upsetting this all was! God what do I do now? The doctor even said he would feel better if I stayed at the hospital a few days for tests, until I could decide to go into assisted living or find someone to live with. I was certainly not ready for this, and no way was I going to stay in the hospital that night, nor even consider going into an assisted living facility! Here went my stubborn side of me. You know, sometimes being stubborn with the things that seem to want to take your life over, is a good thing. Since I was saved, I have leaned on God in every situation, turning to Him for not only comfort, but guidance. He, alone, knows what is best for me. The doctor's say what they think is best, but we need to feel it in our own hearts and desire what God wants for us, then move forward.

I went home, dreading, knowing I must tell my family. I didn't call my daughter till the next day. Why upset her at night. I just went to bed. Morning came, I had to make the calls. Not easy. Of course, my daughter was upset because I didn't call her or anyone; and I didn't allow the hospital to make any calls either. I was feeling better now, I felt I would be okay, if I did what the doctor said, and stop all I was doing for awhile, and see my doctor as well. I have not always done things in a timely manner, I tend to be a bit compulsive, especially when it comes to decisions. If I feel a peace, I move forward on it, and also when it seems I have no choice. At times, though, some things done compulsively come back to bite you. Yet God has always had a purpose, maybe a learning experience, but still a purpose for everything I have been through.

For a couple of weeks, both weekends, a wonderful Christian couple, friends of mine for 30 some years, picked me up and brought me to their home in Rhode Island. They offered to have me move into their basement apartment. She was going to be home working, so there would always be someone home, especially at night. Her husband was going to be traveling with his job a lot, and we'd be company for each other. I never dreamed God would move me back to my home state, ever. I was so comfortable each time I was there. Again, I moved forward . . . this time for health reasons and knowing I would be company for my friend. Her husband was thrilled also. They and my family helped with all the moving. Of course, my daughter made all the final decorating of my apartment, like she usually does. She's always there when I need her. I, once again, settled in, found a new church family, and things seemed to be going well.

Some time passed and things started changing in the home. I started feeling uncomfortable with my friend seeming upset with me at times. I sensed the tension increasing between us.

My restlessness became more frequent. Signs were becoming more evident that more change was coming to my life. CHOICES, right or wrong, we have to face them and possibly suffer the consequences. But, I knew God had a plan. I knew I moved there for a few reasons. I loved my friends dearly; yet felt so strongly in my heart it was getting near time for another change in my life. This had been another learning experience for three friends of many years. I prayed to God to show me what to do next.

I received a phone call from Prudy, my best friend from Florida, and she asked me to go on a trip with her across the southern states. This was on a Thursday and she had no idea what was going on in my life. She sensed I was hesitant, and asked what else I had to do that I couldn't take two months off. So . . . . drop everything and come to Florida. Within a split second, I decided to go! She was amazed and said "You mean you're going to come with me?!". I did say, "If I get to Florida, I may not want to come back." She commented, "well, that is all up to God for sure, if that is His plan for you."

I left for Florida the very next day! I called my family to let them know I'd be gone for two months and I also let my friend know. Circumstances change no matter where we are. I arrived in Florida at Prudy's house while we waited to leave on Monday. She got bad news about the condo she was renting. The trip was going to have to be postponed. Monday came, and she had business to tend to; so I went to Saint Cloud, to the trailer park I used to live in, to visit some friends. I was good friends with the manager and shared with her the happenings of the past year . . . and how it all lead me back down here. She began to tell me that she had two new places, completely renovated, and up for sale. We discussed the financial aspects in renting with an option to buy. It was truly affordable for me. So another step forward took place.

I moved, and and Florida became my permanent home once again. Loved being back, but still felt the home I chose was only temporary, and mentioned that to the manager. Got myself settled and soon found my home church, Eastern Avenue Baptist Church. All was well with my soul as it usually is when I follow God's plan and will for me.

Yes, this decision caused some problems and some hurt feelings because I tend to do things quickly. My daughter is used to it since it's happened all her life. At first, it's difficult to accept changes when they come on quickly but soon we all knew I was supposed to be here. Eventually God opened doors of opportunity to serve Him in new ways.

While living at St. Cloud Trailer Park, I later faced a very sad experience. My Service Dog, Timmy, seemed to be acting very weak. I took him to the vet to have him checked. I was told his heart was failing. Congestive heart failure and his age was against him. He was 11 years old now.

He would be surprised if he made it through the summer months. I, of course, was very upset. Another tragedy about to hit me. I k new he was getting older, and he did have a heart murmur all his life. But are we ever prepared for it? The vet suggested I call the school to prepare the school to find a Service Dog for me. I went home crying out to God, help me, I need your intervention to get through this one! Called my prayer team at church to pray with me; and began to take the steps with the school. Not having money for the school,

I had no idea how this was going to come to pass. I had to put all my trust and faith in my God, who has never failed me yet, and never will. A month later and Timmy was getting worse. He developed a cough, that would put him outstretched on the floor to catch his breath. Nell, at the school called me often, about different dogs she went to look at, or heard about, but they never seemed like the right one for me. She knew me well and knew I preferred a poodle, but it may not be possible to find one and get him trained in time. So, she was also in prayer to find one in which we would make a good team. Waiting still and praying. Time went by, and I went out less and less because Timmy was unable to walk very far. It was getting difficult, and I felt so badly for him that he be so sick and still have to work with me! God knows well our needs and promises to answer every one of them. Knowing and believing that, I waited, yet at times impatiently to be honest with you.

I even thought that God maybe thinks I don't really need a service dog anymore. Checked with my doctor, and he affirmed the need was still there. The dog and medication were keeping the attacks at bay, until God does the healing. Sometimes I feel that some things in life, we have to accept and not let them stop us, and use all for His glory and praise.

It happened one day . . . . the call came. It was Nell. She felt she had found "a gift from heaven" for me. It was out of town, but she wanted to check with me before making the trip, to be sure I wanted him. He was a white poodle, bigger than Timmy was and fully trained. Did I ever get excited. She also said they would have two fund raisers to meet the cost of the dog, who was being purchased from another school in Florida. We met in Orlando that afternoon. She got out of the car, and pulled Nell as she ran to me. She said, he sure didn't do that for me when I went to get him! This surely looked promising. I put him in the car with Timmy. When we got adjusted to each other, they would see what more training he may need, so the school could certify him. It didn't take much and he was mine.

The day after I took him home, it seemed the two dogs got along very well. Sitting on my couch, with one on each side of me. Timmy seemed to become very passive quickly. Kind of like taking a back seat and letting Brodie take the lead and follow me around. The next day, I decided to take them d to the lake front, to see if I was going to be able to handle getting around with two dogs. I got them in the car just fine. Both being very obedient, they ran to the car and jumped in, only with the command, let's go bye bye. I didn't quite make it to the lakefront when Brodie kept coming up to me and tapping his foot on my arm. Not ever being signaled by him, I wasn't sure what was going on. Then he would go to the back seat again, and back to me. I pulled over and stopped the car. Thinking he would then jump on my lap while I took a pill. Nope he went to the back again! Oh, I thought . . . . why isn't Timmy coming up to me? I sat there, holding my breath for a minute, to give me the strength to get out and go to the back seat. Sure enough, Timmy had died in my back seat! Oh, I was so sad, yet a part of me was relieved. Strange feeling to have. He looked so peaceful, as Brodie licked his face seeming to try to revive him. I held him and gave him a kiss goodbye. I had a plan with friends of mine, that when this did happen, to call them immediately. I did so, and they came with two cars. He took Timmy in his truck to bury him on his large property at their home. His wife took me and Brodie to her home for me to calm down and have some tea with her, so I wouldn't have to go home and be alone. I held on to Brodie as he laid on my lap to comfort me. A true gift from God were both dogs to me.

Brodie and I bonded quickly, went for a little more training, and I taught him at home also, as I had with Timmy. He learned well and certainly took an interest in watching over me. He past and was certified by the same school Timmy was. The fund raisers brought in almost enough to cover the costs for him, and my wonderful church family at Eastern Avenue Baptist Church helped supply what would have had to come out of my pocket, and taken who knows how long to pay it off! To them I am truly grateful. Now I see, once again, how God provides ALL my needs, all the time. If you ever wonder why He is not answering you, Check out if your priorities are within His will or not. If they are, He will always answer, not always how you think or want Him to, but He will answer with what is best for you at the time. Another adventure in faith.

Soon after, it was getting close to making a decision as to whether or not I was going to buy the trailer home I was living in. I still didn't feel I was suppose to. Where was I going to go? Seeking God's will once again, and as usual waited expectantly for His leading.

Within the next month, I was in Walgreen's pharmacy speaking with the saleslady in the photo department. She was sharing that she had recently moved into a 55+ mobile home community that was affordable for her. She also said there were other mobile homes for sale and selling at a great price. I immediately got the address and went to look into it. The manager took me around to looks at those the park were selling. They needed repair, yet the going price was tempting. Walked out of the office a bit disappointed, wondering why I was there. A gentleman met me outside the office and told me to ride around and look into those that had for sale signs in their window. I did just that. Went to look at two, and they were much too expensive for me. A lady and her mom spoke with me, and I shared a bit about how I felt God was leading me to find a home. They looked at each other, and the daughter told me to wait a minute, she needed to make a phone call. After the call she showed me where I needed to go to look at another mobile home. I drove over to it, and an older couple were waiting in their florida room for me. I walked in and they both gave me hugs, as Christians do when they meet, even for the first time. The home was in beautiful condition and they said they were anxious to get back to their northern home.

After looking through the home, she asked if I liked it. I was so excited! She asked me how soon could I move in. Yes, you guessed it, within the week I was moving. Best thing yet, It ended up not costing me anything! Another gift from my loving God, and the beautiful couple, Barbara and Tony, he brought me to.! I will never forget them.

More excitement and another wonderful gift came to me later that year. My granddaughter and her husband blessed me with Great Grandson, Oliver Samuel. Oh what a joy floods my soul, once again.

It is very exciting to watch a legacy grow. I was so grateful that he was healthy and a happy baby as Naomi was. Couldn't wait to see him. Pictures flooded my email. I knew I wouldn't get to see him till the summer came around, and I was able to go north to visit.

Summer came, and I was able to spend three months in New England. God opened doors for me to visit family and friends, staying a time here and there in their homes. I got to see my new Great Grandson Oliver, and to my surprise, he let me hold him and I began to feel a bond settling in. As family we enjoyed each other with all the family events that usually take place in the summer months. With Great Grandchildren now, I especially enjoyed that I was elected to stay with them, while the adults went on all the rides at amusement parks, or went swimming. What fun it was, and what wonderful memories we made together. I will never forget it, and pray we have many more summers to do the same. What a blessing it is!.

A year and 8 months later, another GREAT grandson, Silas Elliot was born! Another pride and joy comes into my life! It is so exciting to look forward to my summer vacations, and to watch another generation growing up before my eyes. They grow up so fast. To see all my grandchildren all grown up now, is amazing to me. I still have one younger Granddaughter, Sage. She and Great Grand daughter, Naomi are close in age, and are already school age. So they are growing before my eyes also. Time move so fast, it is hard for me to believe sometimes, and yet I can't help being so grateful for the blessings of family, and the love they bestow on me, and the patience and understanding they have for me. It is certainly something to cherish and thank God for. He is certainly a blessing from God.

In Memory of Timmy, my 1st Service Dog
2001-2011

My Service Dog Now, Brodie

CHAPTER XVII

YOU TOO CAN SAY: NOW I SEE

How could I have been in God's will with all the negative things I allowed to control my life? I finally got so tired and worn out from being confused and deceived, I knew I needed to change. I had gotten to a place I did not even know myself anymore. I knew confusion was not from God. I have always had confidence when I walk with God. A minister friend once said, "You hold the reigns, but let God do the driving." I wonder why any of us want to go our own way and not God's way? When I'm living a self-centered life, then it cannot be God-centered. I can get off track when I am not letting God have full control. It is a dangerous place to be. There is such a peace when walking with God, and knowing I am in His care. His way always makes me feel secure, content and full of joy. What more should any of us want?

I have complicated my life so many times thinking I needed to live a certain way. All the time, I was pleasing people or conforming to what I thought was expected of me.

I have said all this to say, I have had choices. Now I see who I am and why I experienced all that I did. I may have slid down other paths at times, yet always chose to please God with the life He gave me. Even when I went off the path He chose for me, He used it for His glory . . . once I got back on track, that is. We can choose to do anything we want to do. The enemy of our souls will oblige us with temptations to lead us down wrong paths, and circumstances that force us into living certain ways. As a young person, our curiosities can drive us into directions not pleasing to God. I believe my folks taught me well; that God cares about what we do, more than even our parents. I am thankful for the foundation that was laid down for me by my parents. Hearing the Word at church and Sunday school as a child instilled a strong consciousness of God's presence. He knows all and sees all. Yet for years I did not know I could have a personal relationship with God. 4 He desires for all to know Him in a personal way. By giving your life to Jesus, the grace of God can and will set you free from the bondages of sin and spiritual death. (Romans 3:23,24) says: "for all have sinned and fall short of the glory of God, being justified freely by His grace through the redemption that is in Christ Jesus." I don't know how anyone's life can change for the better without God's intervention. All He asks is that we confess we are sinners, in need of our Savior, and ask Jesus to come into our lives. When we surrender our lives to Him, we actually give up, stop, let go and let God take over. What He feels needs changing in us, we will then desire to be changed also in those areas. We allow Jesus to be Lord of our lives and then we see, through the working of His Holy Spirit in us, what the purpose for our being created was all about.

No matter how bad you think you are or how far from God you feel, He loves you. He loved you so much that He let His own Son die for you, that you might have eternal life. (John 3:16, 17) says, "For God so loved the world that He gave His only begotten Son, that whosoever believes in Him should not perish, but have everlasting life. For God sent not His Son into the world to condemn the world, but that the world through Him might be saved." You can experience renewed life right now, right where you are. You have a choice, accept or reject God's free gift of salvation, eternal life through Jesus Christ, His Son. Romans 10:9 says, "If we confess with your mouth the Lord Jesus, and will believe in your heart that God has raised Him from the dead, you will be saved."

Just ask Him to come into your heart and life, and He will. He is waiting for you. That is all He asks of us. He wants to help us stay out of the pitfalls that are out to destroy our lives.

I pray you experience God in His fullness as I have. In the renewing of your spirit, and a new life only He can give you, you will also be able to say, I was once in spiritual darkness, but NOW I SEE!

Sister in law, Bev (center) with part of her family. Hubby Roland, granddaughter Sarah, Daughter Ellen and her hubby Richard, granddaughter Britney.

Main photo: Author meets birth mother.
Small pictures: Youngest sister Dee; brother Rich; niece Brenda, Dee's oldest daughter; niece Robyn and her mom, my sister Joan.

Top picture: Author with daughter's family.
Five children, Jenni, Jeff, Jesse, Mike, Bianca and three
great grands, Naomi, Oliver and Silas.

"Thank God for His Word
His inspired and trustworthy truth
upon which we can build our lives."

Always allow the Bible to be your
first preference for daily reading and study.

It nourishes your spirit and soul.

～

ABOUT THE AUTHOR— WHAT HER FRIENDS SAY

This story is written by Lynnie Lang, an amazing woman, who has a gift from God that encourages others to reach their full potential in Christ. Her books enhance your desire to reach out for all God has to give you, and to learn from His Word. She reminds us to never let other books take the place of daily Bible reading; as Scripture is a living document telling you how to practice faith in daily life, when you do what it says.

Lynnie is a "small town" lady with a big heart. She was born and grew up in the state of Rhode Island, but her life journeys have taken her far beyond this tiny state in New England. She is the mother of two adult children, grandmother of six, at the time this book was originally written, now also a great grandmother of three. She has been a foster mother to many over the years.

Lynnie was the founder and first president of the Warwick, Rhode Island Chapter of Woman's Aglow Fellowship, an international Christian woman's organization. She worked in the nursing profession while living in Rhode Island, and as a nurse/officer at Orange County Corrections in Florida. Trained in Christian counseling, she has also directed a home for women in addiction recovery. She now resides in St. Cloud, Florida. Busy in outreach for lost souls in prisons, nursing homes and on the streets. Enjoys life, family, church family, friends; loves to write and encourage others to allow her books to enrich the desire of those who read them to always dig deeper into God's Word; to learn the truths on how to overcome the evil in this world, and walk the spiritual walk He intended for our lives.